# MATCH FISHING
## A Champion's Guide

# MATCH FISHING
## A Champion's Guide

**KIM MILSOM**

The Crowood Press

First published in 1994 by
The Crowood Press Ltd
Ramsbury, Marlborough
Wiltshire SN8 2HR

**British Library Cataloguing-in-Publication Data**

A catalogue record for this book is available from the British Library.

ISBN 1 85223 791 0

**Picture Credits**
All photographs by the author except for those on pages 2, 26 (right),
29, 35, 38, 43 (bottom), 54, 55 (both), 64, 68, 69, 77, 80 (left), 84,
95, 100 and 107 which are by Matthew Greaves; those on pages 26
(left), 50, 101 and 121 which are by Gary Barclay; those on pages 71
and 88 which are by Brian McCarrick; that on page 6 which is by L.
Roberts; that on page 82 which is by Martin Phillips; and that on page
106 which is by Andrew Jones.
Colour photographs are reproduced by courtesy of *Improve Your Coarse
Fishing*.
Line drawings by P. Groombridge.

Phototypeset by Intype, London
Printed and bound in Great Britain by BPC Hazell Books Ltd.
A member of The British Printing Company Ltd.

# CONTENTS

# INTRODUCTION

Angling is well known as being one of the country's biggest participation sports and, as with any other sport, many of the participants are competitive by nature. This, in many cases, will eventually prompt them to try their luck at match fishing, a branch of the sport which can be frustrating for both newcomers and experienced match anglers alike. The rules set by the fish appear to change from week to week and this, combined with the element of luck introduced by the drawbag, makes the sport one of the most complicated and difficult ones to succeed at. But these very problems mean that success becomes all the more satisfying. Numerous skills are required in order to achieve any consistency; a good match angler never stops learning. Continual improvement is necessary for everyone, beginners and world champions alike.

Books like this become one of the best aids when looking for short cuts to success, since they contain knowledge essential for any angler looking to improve. I know, because I read every match fishing book published. If I pick up just one decent tip from a book, which gives me just one more result, then I will have won back more than the cost of the book! Most match anglers will, of course, pick up far more than one good idea from a book.

This book contains my thoughts and ideas on most of the methods that I use when competing on the big match circuit. But you will probably notice that despite the sport being so complicated, I always try to use comparatively simple ideas and techniques to catch my fish. My methods should be easy enough for the beginner to understand, as well as the expert.

I have been taking part at various levels of

*Just a part of the author's collection of trophies.*

competitive angling for over twenty years now, and during that time I have gradually seen huge changes in the methods used. For example, twenty years ago few books would have mentioned pole fishing. Now pole fishing is so important that it requires several chapters to cover the subject; indeed, it would not have been difficult to devote a whole book to it. There is, of course, far more to match fishing than just poles, and this book is intended for everyone, no matter what types of venue, or style, they prefer.

My intention is to condense the most useful and important ideas, from my twenty years of experience, into the pages of this book. Then everyone who reads it will, it is hoped, improve and become more successful at their own match angling.

# 1 THINK FOR SUCCESS

This book should help you catch fish no matter what level of match angling, or indeed pleasure angling, you are involved at. Whether you take it seriously, or fish strictly for fun, it is still nice to be able to catch more fish. But before discussing the various methods required to consistently tempt your quarry, let us consider how to be successful from a different, and not so obvious angle.

Fishing involves many different skills and these can be learnt, with practice, by most people. But as well as perfecting the various float-fishing and legering-type skills, it is very important to be able to work out which ones are most likely to be successful on a particular day. It sounds obvious, but is it?

The majority of match anglers follow the crowd and fish using the accepted methods for a particular water, without really trying to think up a more successful set of tactics. I always try to work out two things: a) roughly what weight will be needed to win, or at least get in the frame, and b) what is the easiest way to catch that weight?

I have taken this approach throughout my career, always looking for the easiest way to succeed. Examples are always a good way to illustrate a point, and you will find them used regularly throughout this book; now we can go back in time to my early days in competitive angling, when I was a junior with my local club, to explain what I mean.

Many of the local club matches were held on stretches of the upper Thames. At this time it held a decent head of chub, roach and bream, and everyone used to fish for these. But the angling skills on show in the local club had their limitations and few of these fish were caught. Two or three pounds was usually a big weight.

Now, it had not escaped my attention that as well as the larger species, which everyone targeted, there was also a thriving population of bleak and gudgeon, which were much easier to catch. Three pounds was likely to win, and was easily achievable with bleak or gudgeon from a very high percentage of the pegs. I was not particularly efficient at catching them but, given five hours, I could come up with the appropriate weight.

I quickly started to win a large number of these club events, which did not always go down too well with some of the senior members I was beating! I was not winning by out-fishing them using their methods, but simply by out-thinking them when it came to choice of tactics.

Incidentally, during part of this period I was winning with gudgeon caught on the straight lead. My float-fishing skills did not extend to fishing on the bottom without the float continually dragging under! However, by developing my own style of catching them on the straight lead, using a 4in (10cm) tail to get the bait down quickly, I was able to put together catches of, at times, over 300 fish.

Another good way to learn quickly and improve your skills is to swap ideas with other anglers. The best time to talk to a stranger is after he has just won, since most anglers will be happy to tell others how they did it while they are celebrating their moment of triumph. But to learn more quickly, on a regular basis, I would suggest travelling to matches with one or two other anglers, who want to fish at the same level as you. If you pool your new knowledge after the match, or on the way home, you will be able to improve at a much faster rate than if you are just trying to learn by yourself. Two or three heads are better than one.

My club match wins with bleak and gudgeon demonstrate the kind of thinking which can keep you one step in front of the opposition. I am now going to use a more extended example to show how new winning methods developed on a water with which I am probably associated more than any other – the Gloucester Canal. Running through the various tactical changes the canal has seen during my open match career should be both instructive and, it is hoped, interesting.

## DEVELOPING WAYS TO CATCH SKIMMERS

I will begin back in 1977 when I had my first open win on the venue. This victory came on the Hempsted length of the canal and it is this stretch I am going to concentrate on at the moment.

*A skimmer bream is guided towards the net.*

That win was achieved with a catch of skimmer bream, taken on the tip, using a straight-lead rig in those days before swimfeeders caught on. Feeding was done by hand, with balls of pure bread groundbait containing squatts or pinkies. Hookbait was usually the extra-soft, home-bred maggots better known as gozzers.

In summer virtually everyone fished for bream, and they could be caught from many areas. The best way to catch them was to overcast the feed area and then 'twitch' the hookbait back towards you. Bites would often come soon after the bait had resettled and on some days a surprisingly high number of fish would be on the hook when the bait was moved, without a bite having registered.

Over the next couple of seasons the feeding was modified; smaller, softer balls were fed by catapult in an attempt to avoid scaring the quarry. The straight-lead/twitch method was still used and stood me in good stead for several years. But then, experimentation on a day when I was struggling to catch discovered a better way of catching the skimmers.

This was the August bank holiday in 1980, during an open match which was run by Gloucester United Anglers. I had drawn very well, on Hempsted bend, which must be one of the more famous areas in match fishing. However, on this occasion, my joy at drawing a good peg was short-lived, as two and a half hours into the event I had only about 1½lb of fish in the net and the peg was dead. Those around me were also struggling, and the situation was not promising.

Rather than give up I had decided that I had nothing to lose by experimenting, so I took the decision to try a feeder, which was still not accepted as a productive method on the canal. I decided to use a small block-end feeder, full of squatts, rather than an open-end version with groundbait. My choice was to pay off.

After half a dozen casts the fish turned up. At first the bites were small taps, many of which were probably fish bumping into the line or feeder. But, gradually, proper bites developed and my catch rate grew. The skimmers were of small average size, but by the end of the match I had put close to thirty of them into the net, to win with 14lb 9½oz. Many of the fish fell to two or three squatts on the hook, a ploy which I had discovered earlier, during hookbait experiments on the straight lead.

During the following summer the small block-end feeder full of squatts kept me in the frame on a regular basis. I discovered that it was still best to spend the first hour or two on the straight lead, feeding groundbait by catapult, and then change over. By just picking up odd fish early on it was possible to settle the shoal down and then catch heavily when the switch to a feeder was made.

Many other anglers started using feeders; but they nearly all went for open-end versions with groundbait from the start. They tended to catch early on but then fade. I usually overtook them later, so I stayed with my method.

It is worth mentioning at this point that the legering methods that I developed on the Gloucester Canal were used to great effect on other venues. The Exeter Canal is the classic example; friends and I started visiting it for close season opens and, by using our Gloucester Canal methods, we won a high percentage of the matches. Most methods can be successfully adapted to more than one venue.

## FISHING FOR ROACH AND BREAM

During the summer of 1981 far more anglers were starting to try out poles. Many of them would try pole fishing for the last couple of hours if they had failed to catch bream. Often they would catch two or three pounds of roach, on maggots, during these late stages of the day. I watched these developments with interest. I

*Alan Scotthorne, a highly successful match angler himself, unhooks a fish at the Holme Pierrepont rowing course venue in Nottingham.*

was still very successful with my skimmer fishing, but they were not quite as abundant as they had been; 7lb or 8lb would nearly always frame and sometimes win. What sort of weights would be possible if roach were fished for properly all match? I decided that the next time I drew poorly for bream, I would find out.

My first serious, all-out, summer-time assault on the roach took place during the second weekend of the 1982 season. I drew an early number, opposite the rowing club (for those of you familiar with the venue), and pole fished all day to win with over 9lb of decent roach. I was not the only angler to be showing an interest in the roach, but I was certainly one of the first to prove that they could beat bream. I was one step in front of the crowd again.

It was noticeable at this time that roach usually took time to respond to any angler's loosefeed, so I developed my tactics to take this into account. It became my standard summer-time approach to start off fishing for bream,

while loosefeeding on a pole line for roach. I also abandoned the block-end feeder with squatts. I mentioned earlier that bream responded more quickly to an open-end feeder, so I used them instead. I was not concerned about the risk of the bream leaving part way through the match: as the match progressed roach would become my main target.

So I learnt to make the most of two areas of the canal. Often I would swap between the two areas all match: as soon as the roach slowed up I would move to the bream and vice versa. Sometimes I ended up with mostly roach, on other occasions bream would dominate: often it would be a fifty-fifty mix. The proportions did not matter; what was important was that I was coming up with a good weight nearly every time.

I suspect that many pegs were capable of 6lb of skimmers if they were fished for all match, or 6lb of roach if they were fished for. By swapping between the two species I would often end up

*A powerful roach/bream hybrid finally gives up at Worsborough Reservoir, Barnsley.*

with 4lb of skimmers and 4lb of roach. Building a decent weight was much easier with this approach: remember what I said earlier about always looking for the easiest ways to succeed!

## EXPERIMENTING WITH BLOODWORMS

All good things eventually come to an end, and this approach was no exception. By 1985 a dramatic change had taken place on the canal: nearly all of the commercial boat traffic stopped. Without the big ships using the canal its waters lost a lot of their colour. The quality roach all but stopped feeding in the clear water, as did most of the skimmers, and weights dropped. Enter the bloodworm!

I was certainly not the first angler to start using bloodworms on the canal: several other anglers had been using them for a couple of years. But the top weights they were achieving were not big enough to worry me while I could still catch quality fish on maggots. In 1985 that situation changed. The winning weights dropped and came within range of the small fish hauls, which were falling to bloodworms. It became obvious that I needed to change baits to win on a regular basis, so I searched out a supply of worms and started experimenting.

My first attempt at fishing the canal with bloodworms in a match saw me fail to win my section by a few ounces. On my next attempt I finished third overall, but this was overshadowed by my third try, which resulted in a win. This was achieved with over 200 fish, mostly gudgeon and ruffe, which weighed 6lb 4½oz. I fished just 5 yards (or metres) from the bank and fed the bloodworms in a mixture of pure bread groundbait and ground hemp.

This approach was to prove successful until 1987. By this time the population of gudgeon and ruffe had declined dramatically and it was much more difficult to build a weight of them. Visiting anglers, though, were catching more roach on bloodworms, something which I was struggling to do.

More experimenting was needed, so a group of us started to try out the range of continental-type groundbaits that were being used by the visiting anglers, since these seemed to hold the key to catching the roach. By sitting in a line, and all using different mixes, we homed in on the most successful groundbait for the canal's roach and skimmers. It took a while, but we got there.

The best approach was to feed half a dozen orange-sized balls of groundbait at the start of a session, then top up with smaller balls as required, usually after the first hour and a half. The roach went for this in a big way and I managed winning weights of up to 15lb of them. Again, it is worth mentioning that the groundbait and feeding pattern to which the Gloucester roach succumbed was used with great success, for the same species, on other venues. This approach continued to be a winner through 1988 and 1989, though it was not always allowed. If bloodworms were banned, I simply reverted back to my old, two-pronged maggot attack.

However, the 1990 season heralded another change in the fish's feeding habits. Bloodworms were allowed, but for the first two matches of the season I struggled, catching only a limited number of small fish. During the course of these events I noticed that odd decent roach were falling to other anglers who were fishing maggots. It was time for some more experimenting.

After the second match I moved further along the canal to have a quick evening practice session. I piled in bloodworms in groundbait, but then loosefed maggots over the top of it. I caught small fish on bloodworms for a while, then tried swapping to maggots on the hook. The difference was incredible: after three hours I had 15lb of roach in the net. The quality fish had reverted back to maggots. Another lesson learnt: just because bloodworms are allowed does not mean that they are the best bait.

The following weekend I returned to Hempsted for a match. Again I started by feeding bloodworms in groundbait, but this time I also fed maggots over the top. After an hour of struggling for small fish on bloodworms, I changed hookbaits to maggot. I won with half an ounce short of 20lb. Again I had quickly found a new winning method.

It lasted for just two seasons. It was still a winner in 1991, but at the start of the 1992 campaign it failed. Fortunately, however, my habit of continuing to feed bloodworms (or jokers by this time) at the start meant that I found the new winning style immediately. By changing back to bloodworms on the hook, I still managed to win my first Gloucester Canal match of the 1992 season – though admittedly it was not at Hempsted.

The bigger roach had, for some unexplained reason, all but vanished. In their place, however, were masses of small roach along with perch, gudgeon and ruffe, which averaged around twenty to the pound, and could be caught from most of the pegs. A practice session quickly revealed that the most efficient way of catching them was to start at 3 yards (or metres) and then go out to 6 to 7 yards (or metres). Bream and skimmers could also still be caught in some areas, but these demanded a different approach. They showed little interest in bloodworms and were best fished for at longer range with maggots and squatts.

This up-to-date situation will probably only last for a season or two so I will be keeping my eyes open for new developments. Then, when my current tactics show signs of failing, I shall endeavour to be among the first anglers to establish what the new winning methods are, and change to them quickly to try to keep one step in front of the opposition.

*A double-figure catch from the Gloucester Canal at Hempsted.*

You will have noticed just how often winning methods can change, sometimes quite drastically. Back in 1977, if someone had told me that I would be winning on the canal with poles and bloodworms, it would have sounded unlikely to say the least. Always try to think out ways of improving your fishing and look closely at new ideas, rather than following the crowd. Winning then becomes a lot simpler. It is also much easier when you know as much as possible about the various methods which match fishing can demand. Much of that knowledge will be supplied by the following chapters, so read on.

# 2 WAGGLER FISHING

Many floats come under this heading, as 'waggler' describes virtually any float which is attached to the line bottom end only. Most wagglers will be made from peacock quill, though many other materials are also in use: the most notable being balsawood which is in common use for the smaller versions of the float used on canals.

So what are the main reasons for using a waggler instead of a float attached by both ends? What are its main advantages (and disadvantages) compared to its rivals?

To start with, the weight around the base of the float gives it great stability and helps prevent wind and surface drift moving it off line. In light winds a large top-and-bottom float could be used instead: but, unless the bulk of the shotting required can be placed well down the line, top-and-bottom floats can result in lots of tangles if fished at distance. On the other hand, when fishing at close range, a float attached by both ends will usually be better than a waggler, as a waggler cannot be held back to slow the bait down to any great extent. A waggler is thus first choice if a float is required to fish beyond pole range in adverse wind conditions, or in good wind conditions when it is important that most of the weight required for casting is close to the float.

One further advantage of a waggler is worth considering, particularly when fishing shallow water: the float causes very little disturbance when a bite is struck, compared to the splash caused by many top-and-bottom floats.

There are several different types of waggler. Here is a guide to deciding what types to use and how to fish them in the various types of waters where they are of use.

## STILLWATER WAGGLER FISHING

### Short-range Fishing

For short-range waggler fishing, whether on lakes or canals, the balsa versions of the float tend to be my first choice. These are usually made with a comparatively thick body towards the bottom of the float and a thin, sensitive tip.

Most of the casting weight required will be used to lock the float. For close-range fishing we are probably looking at using two or three BBs. I always slide tiny lengths of silicone tubing on to the main line before attaching the locking shot. Non-toxic shot can start to damage the line, particularly if moved very often, so I prefer to use the silicone tubing as a cushion, rather than risk any line damage.

The shotting below the float will depend on the depth to be fished. As a general starting rule I would suggest one no. 8 shot (or two no. 10s, which is the same) for each 18in (45cm) of depth; for example, in 6ft (1.8m) of water use four no. 8s or eight no. 10s. I realize that for many anglers, particularly beginners, shotting is a very boring subject, but it is very important. Correct shotting is vital to catch more fish, so ignore it at your peril.

The bottom shot would usually be positioned 12–18in (30–45cm) from the hook and the others would be spread above it, at about 9in (24cm) intervals. I tend to use three no. 10 shot closest to the hook for this type of fishing then the appropriate number of no. 8s above that. At the start of a session I would usually set the float a few inches over depth, so that

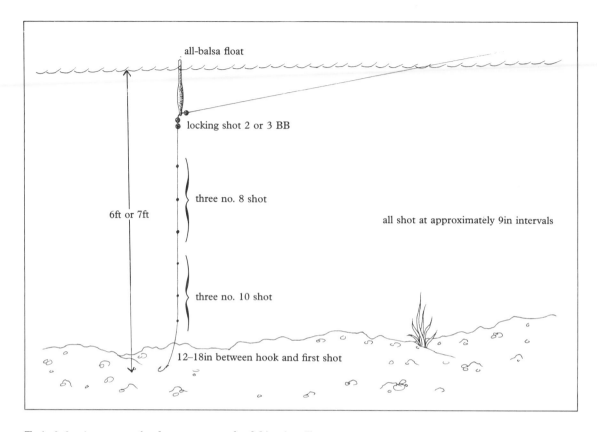

all-balsa float

locking shot 2 or 3 BB

three no. 8 shot

6ft or 7ft

all shot at approximately 9in intervals

three no. 10 shot

12–18in between hook and first shot

*Typical shotting pattern for short-range waggler fishing in still water.*

the bait will fall all the way to the bottom. This shotting pattern will give the bait a nice, slow, natural fall, particularly when it is near the bottom, but adjustments may well be required as the fish start to respond.

One common problem is for the bait to be chewed without a bite registering. If this happens, simply move the shot down the line, closer to the hook. The fish will then have to move less distance, with the bait in its mouth, before it moves a shot and registers a bite. As well as moving shot closer to the hook, make sure that the float is well shotted down. If much float is showing, it will stop a fish moving off with the bait: any sensible fish is going to drop the bait very quickly if it feels the float.

Another problem that often occurs, particularly in warmer weather when the fish are more active, is for the float not to cock properly because fish are grabbing the bait high up in the water. If you are successfully hitting these bites there is little need to change; if you are not hitting them, try shallowing up. However, this problem is often caused by shoals of minute fish, which are hardly worth catching, in which case you will have to deepen off again and move plenty of shot down the line, to try to take the bait quickly down to the bottom where, hopefully, bigger fish will be present. If you need to use a lot more weight down the line, you will have to remove a locking shot to compensate, or put on a bigger float.

## Long-range Fishing

When fishing at longer range on still waters, a larger float will obviously be required. The two or three BB balsa floats are not going to be of

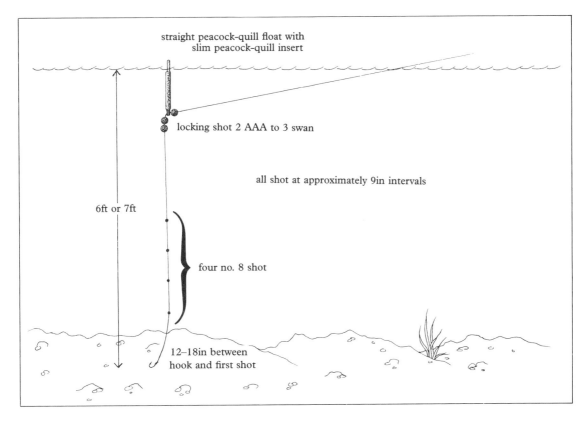

straight peacock-quill float with
slim peacock-quill insert

locking shot 2 AAA to 3 swan

all shot at approximately 9in intervals

6ft or 7ft

four no. 8 shot

12–18in between
hook and first shot

*Typical shotting pattern for long-range waggler fishing in still water of modest depth.*

much use for casting 40 yards (or metres) so I change to peacock-quill floats when fishing at longer ranges; taking from 2 AA–3 swan as conditions dictate. These floats will usually be equipped with a thinner insert at the top to try to keep them sensitive, and if there is much surface drift a long float can be worth considering; here the locking shot act as a kind of stabilizing anchor below the worst of this surface drift. If the surface drift does move the float too much, the hookbait will move and the fish are likely to be very wary of taking it.

The shotting for distance fishing will be very similar to that used closer in, but it is important that you can see when the bottom shot has landed (so that you can tell if a fish has taken the bait on the drop). With the slightly thicker tips, which will be required for the float to be seen at a distance, it is possible that you will

not be able to see when the bottom no. 10 has landed. If this is the case you will need to use no. 8s, closer to the hook, so that bites on the drop, and lift bites, will be easily spotted. In deep water you will probably end up with no. 8s closest to the hook and then no. 6s higher up the line; if fish are feeding near the bottom of 12ft (3.5m) of water it makes sense to use the slightly larger shot to get the bait down to them.

If the fish you are trying to catch insist on feeding on the bottom (which larger species like bream or tench frequently do) it can often be essential to anchor the bait on the bottom and keep it totally still for several minutes at a time. The floats and shotting which I have described so far are designed to catch fish on the drop, or fairly soon after the bait has landed. To keep the bait still on the bottom for

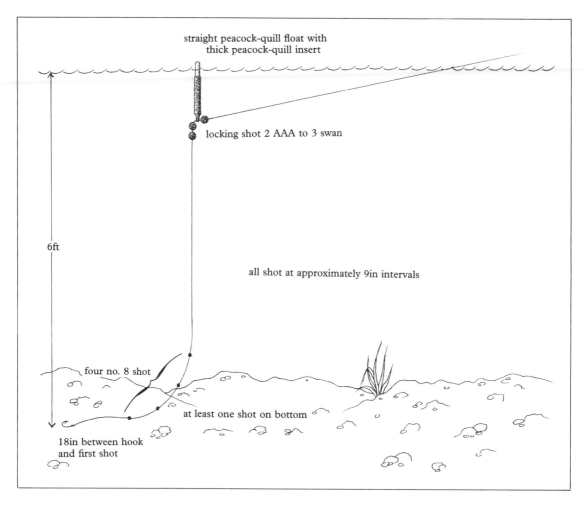

straight peacock-quill float with
thick peacock-quill insert

locking shot 2 AAA to 3 swan

6ft

all shot at approximately 9in intervals

four no. 8 shot

at least one shot on bottom

18in between hook
and first shot

*Waggler rig for keeping the hookbait dead still on lakes affected by gentle tow.*

any length of time requires a slightly different approach.

Even still waters can defy their name by moving to some extent, usually due to the effect of the wind. This means that the float will nearly always be affected by some water movement which will try to drag the bait with it. To fool some of the larger, bottom-feeding fish this dragging has to be stopped completely: we need to anchor the bait by making several adjustments to the tackle. To start with, the shot closest to the hook will be no. 8s since no. 10s will not really be large enough to do the job. The float will be replaced by one with a slightly

thicker tip, so that it will not easily drag under, and finally the depth will be altered so that you are fishing at least 18in (45cm) over depth.

When you cast out, the float will move with the tow, but stop when the shot on the bottom begin to act as a brake or anchor. If the float drags under, remove shot until it does not. If the float still moves with the tow, set it deeper so that more shot are on the bottom. After a few adjustments you should be able to present the hookbait quite still on the bottom. It is also a good idea to hold the rod but also use a rod rest to keep it completely still. The effect of the tow will mean that there is unlikely to be any

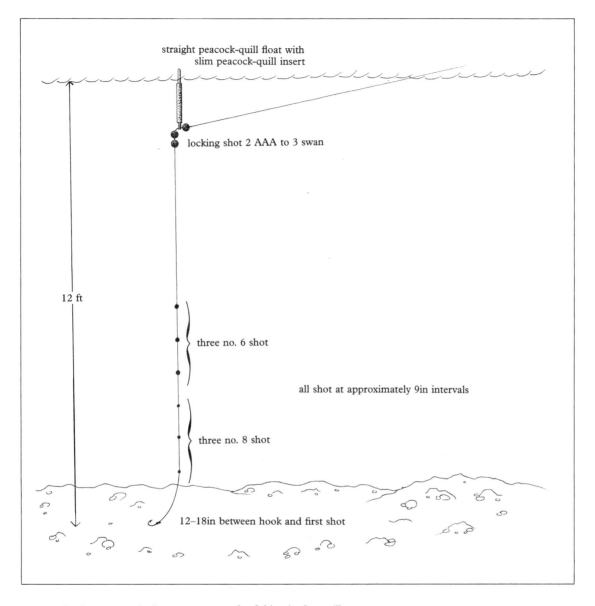

straight peacock-quill float with
slim peacock-quill insert

locking shot 2 AAA to 3 swan

12 ft

three no. 6 shot

all shot at approximately 9in intervals

three no. 8 shot

12–18in between hook and first shot

*Typical shotting pattern for longer-range waggler fishing in deep still water.*

slack line between rod tip and float, so if you move the rod you will pull the float under.

### The Longleat Lakes
An example of using the two types of presentation to good effect, will probably help you to appreciate their benefits. In the mid 1980s the Longleat lakes were among my regular venues.

Three lakes were used for the matches, but for the sake of explaining when to use the different styles, I shall only concentrate on two: the largest lake and the smallest.

The large lake held a huge population of roach, which were active fish, willing to chase after any food which fell in their vicinity. The lightly shotted wagglers, with their inserts, were ideal for catching them. Two different sizes were required, as the lake was much deeper at one end, ranging from about 4–10ft (1.2–3m). For the shallower water a float locked with two AAAs and one BB was used, with three no. 8 shot spread down the line; the fish fed best at quite long range, and a lighter float would not have been effective. In the deeper water a larger float, still with a thin insert, came into play. This would be locked in position with three AAAs and would be shotted with three no. 8s and two or three no. 6s. Both floats would be fished slightly over depth.

To catch the roach, my tackle would be cast to the far edge of the area being fed. The rod would then be dropped into a rest, and I would feed with a catapult. If this was done efficiently I could then pick up the rod again before the bottom shots had landed, so I would be ready to watch for bites. If no bite came within thirty seconds of the bait landing, I would pull the float sharply back towards me a couple of yards, so that the bait would rise from the bottom and fall again on the near edge of the feed area. If no bite came within another thirty seconds I would reel in and repeat the process.

You will have noticed that this is quite an active way of fishing, and also that I gave myself two chances to catch a fish on each cast. This method caught me many double-figure roach weights from Longleat's big lake and, of course, has been used on many other venues with similar effect.

The smaller lake at Longleat held a quite different fish population. Roach were still present but they were smaller, and there tended to be fewer of them. The target species were tench and crucian carp, fish which are much happier picking up bait from the bottom, ideal targets for the over-depth method.

A different float with a much thicker insert was used. It was locked with three AAA shot and, because the lake was shallow, was fished with just three no. 8 shot down the line. The closest was about 15in (38cm) from the hook and the others at 9in (24cm) intervals. A stream flowing through the series of lakes meant that the tow always moved gently in the same direction, but by fishing well over depth the float (and bait) could be kept totally still. Once in position the float would not be moved, so this was a waiting game; the bait would be left in position for five minutes or so before reeling in.

This method produced far fewer bites than the tactics employed on the roach-filled big lake. The size of the target species, however, meant that it was still a winner.

## RIVER WAGGLER FISHING

Slow-flowing rivers can be tackled with similar floats and shotting patterns to still waters. But as rivers become faster, more weight is required down the line to get the bait to the bottom. The floats used are also likely to become thicker-topped in faster flows, particularly if fishing on the bottom.

So in a river with just a gentle flow I will use an insert waggler with no. 8 and/or no. 10 shot at roughly 9in (24cm) intervals on the line. The size of the float will of course vary with the distance to be cast and the strength of the wind. In faster water most of the shot will be increased to no. 6s or even no. 4s; to present the bait properly and, for very pacey rivers, the float will be a straight peacock with no insert. An insert float would vanish every time the bait touched bottom.

Another basic principle to remember on rivers concerns your reel line: it needs to be kept behind the float. If your line overtakes the float, whether because of wind or faster currents between you and the waggler, the float is going to be pulled through the swim at a faster pace than is natural. This will make the hookbait act in a suspicious manner.

The easiest way to overcome this problem is to cast slightly downstream, so that all of the line is behind the float as it begins its journey. In strong winds the line can then be sunk behind the waggler to keep it under control, although sunken lines mean that bites cannot be struck at quite so cleanly. I would suggest sinking the line only when essential. I much prefer to keep the line on the surface and 'mend' it, when necessary, to keep it behind the float. In order to make the line float, simply spray the spool with silicone spray; I use a type meant for dry fly fishing!

Most of my waggler fishing is carried out with a main line sold as 1½lb breaking strain (though tests with a spring balance show that it breaks at over 2lb). It is a 'standard' line, rather than the extra-fine co-polymer types which are available. I use the co-polymers for most of my hooklengths, but I am not yet convinced that they would be able to handle the wear and tear that a main line is subjected to. I also carry spools of stronger main line for use with very heavy floats, or when I am after very large fish. But whenever I can, I use the 1½lb line: there isless resistance when casting, and it is less affected by the wind because of its thinner diameter.

Here follow some examples of how these basic principles can be applied to different river situations.

## Fishing off the Bottom

Catching fish at shallow depths does not necessarily mean that the river lacks depth: many fish, particularly chub and dace, move well off bottom to intercept food. Fishing at full depth can leave you biteless when the peg is actually full of feeding fish. To explain exactly what I mean, here is an example from a practice session on the upper Thames at Kelmscott.

On the day in question I was fishing with a friend and, after a couple of hours, I stopped fishing and walked along the bank to see how he was getting on. He was standing in the water while I stayed at the top of the bank. What I could see from my superior vantage point was very interesting: every time he fed a pouchful of maggots, a mass of large dark shapes would appear from the depths and eat every one. This operation would only take a few seconds, then they would all fade back into the depths.

My friend was fishing at full depth and struggling for bites, so I explained to him what I could see. He shallowed up, cast out and then fed. The fish reappeared but his bait had fallen before the loosefeed arrived – so still no bite.

Eventually we found two ways to solve the problem. Feeding, then casting on top of it, was one method, but this involved the splash of the float right on top of the fish, which could easily scare them. The other way was to overcast, feed, then draw the float and hookbait back into the feed. By doing this 40lb of chub ended up in the keepnet, when we could easily have fished full depth all day and gone home complaining that there were no fish present!

It is unusual for the fish to feed shallow enough actually to be visible, but just think how often this could be happening further below the surface without your realizing it. Varying your depth, and making sure that your hookbait falls through the water with your loosefeed, are two approaches you should always keep in mind.

That same shoal of chub also demonstrated that scaling down to smaller hooks and finer lines can be essential for success. We fished for those chub several times and they gradually became more cautious. Originally we used size 20 hooks and 1½lb hooklengths to catch them, but there came a time when this tackle would produce a few early, quick fish – and then nothing. The fish could still be seen, catching every loose maggot, but they would not touch the hookbait. If the hook was changed to a 22 tied to 1lb line, the difference was incredible: the catch rate was immediately restored, because the more delicate tackle fooled the fish. If you fish venues which see a lot of angling pressure, take this into account and scale down if you are not catching. This applies particularly in very clear water.

Feeding on the waggler, or indeed on any other method, will also vary. The species being sought will often have a great bearing on this. Some species, chub and carp in particular, will consume vast quantities of bait; heavy feeding will sometimes provoke them into a feeding frenzy when they become far more confident

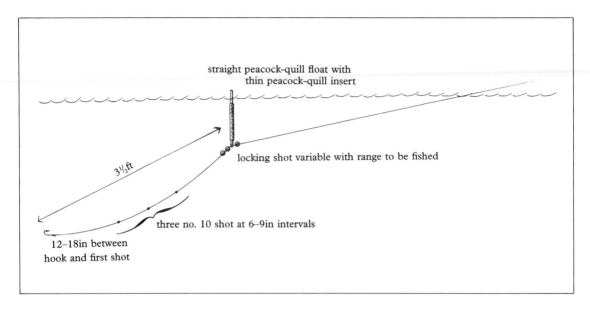

straight peacock-quill float with
thin peacock-quill insert

locking shot variable with range to be fished

3½ft

three no. 10 shot at 6–9in intervals

12–18in between
hook and first shot

*Typical waggler rig for fish feeding close to the surface.*

and easy to catch. Other species, roach in particular, often have to be treated more cautiously, as the following example shows.

Near Stroud there is a small river called the Frome, which contains roach. The river tends to be very clear, and I used to stand on a bridge, armed with maggots, and learn from feeding a shoal I could see. I would start by throwing in half a dozen maggots at a time. At first these would be ignored, but eventually a member of the shoal would start to feed. One by one the others would join in until eventually they were all feeding. Once they were feeding I would try throwing in larger quantities of maggots, but the fish nearly always scattered and refused to eat them. It would then take several minutes of gentle feeding to start them off again. I learnt a lesson: not all fish will accept heavy feeding.

### Fishing on the Bottom

I have talked so far about fishing off bottom. Now let us consider fishing on the bottom in shallow rivers. If you are going to fish with the bait just tripping bottom then the same insert waggler, well shotted down, will still work. However, if you need to slow the bait down by fishing well over depth, you need either to remove shot so that more insert shows, or swap to a different float with a thicker tip to drag line plus shot along the bottom.

To do this, it is essential that you use float adaptors when fishing the waggler. It is also a good idea to carry floats with identical shot-carrying capacities, but different tip thicknesses. Then swapping floats only takes a few seconds. I also make sure that I carry floats that enable me to change to a larger or smaller waggler by changing only one locking shot; for example, if I am using a float which locks with two AA and one BB and takes five no. 8s down the line, there will also be floats in my box locking with three AAA and taking five no. 8s. If my initial choice of float is wrong, or if the weather changes, I can change without wasting time.

A lot of bottom fishing with a waggler will be done in winter. During the hotter summer months the fish tend to be more active, feeding off bottom on far more occasions. This is only a rough guide, however: winter fish, chub in particular, can still decide to feed at any depth.

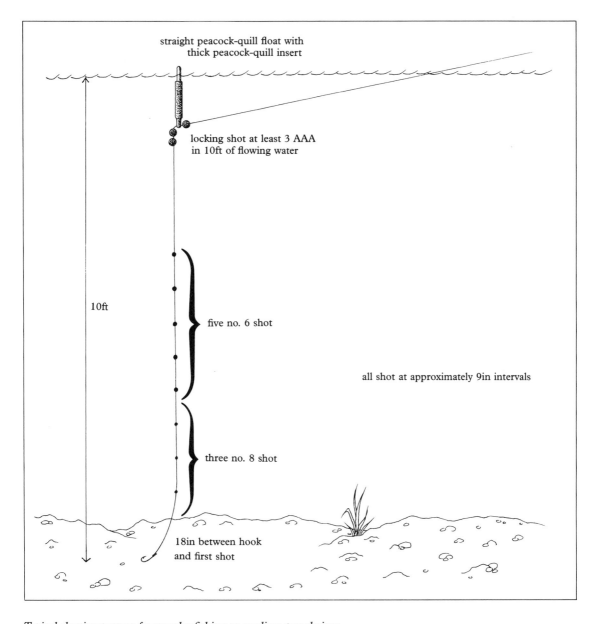

straight peacock-quill float with
thick peacock-quill insert

locking shot at least 3 AAA
in 10ft of flowing water

10ft

five no. 6 shot

all shot at approximately 9in intervals

three no. 8 shot

18in between hook
and first shot

*Typical shotting pattern for waggler fishing on medium-paced river.*

As you start to fish on the bottom in deeper water, you will of course need to use more weight down the line. If you were to use three no. 10 shot in 12ft (3.5m) of water, you would be wasting an awful lot of time while the bait sank and, if your peg was not very long, you might well be reeling in before the bait lands.

In slow-moving water the stillwater principle of one no. 8 for every 18in (45cm) of depth will still be useful. But as the flows being tackled increase, so must the shot size; there comes a point where no. 8s will have to be replaced by no. 6s, or even 4s, though I would still spread them up the line at similar (9in/24cm) intervals. Also bear in mind that, as the flow increases, thicker-topped floats will need to be employed, particularly if you need to drag the bottom in order to slow the bait down. Sensitivity is not a problem in really fast water, as the float will vanish as soon as a fish stops the bait: there is no time for the fish to feel the float and reject the bait.

Obviously faster water will put more strain on your hooks and lines when you are playing large fish, so take this into account when tackling up. The faster water will give fish very little time to inspect the bait, so stronger tackle should still attract bites.

Feeding may also need to be modified in fast water, particularly if it is deep. It can sometimes

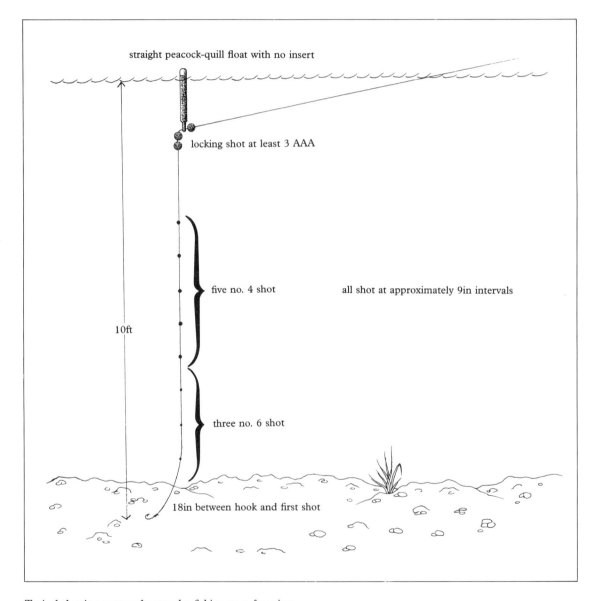

straight peacock-quill float with no insert

locking shot at least 3 AAA

10ft

five no. 4 shot

all shot at approximately 9in intervals

three no. 6 shot

18in between hook and first shot

*Typical shotting pattern for waggler fishing on a fast river.*

be essential to feed well upstream, so that the bait lands within the confines of your peg. It is no good feeding directly in front of you if the feed is landing in the next angler's peg and building a shoal of feeding fish there. With this is mind, keep an eye on the angler upstream of you if the river is fast. If you think that his loosefeed is landing in your peg, make sure that you are fishing at the same range as him. If he has attracted fish to part of your peg you may as well take full advantage of it!

Another common occurrence to watch out for is a shoal of fish which feed quite close to where your feed is being introduced, rather than where it is landing. I suspect that they rise off bottom to intercept the feed as it passes over them, then sink back down. Now, in theory, fishing well off bottom should be the best way to catch these, but if that does not work, they will sometimes fall for a bait fished at full depth; so do not ignore that possibility, particularly if the species involved is roach.

Of course, some fish will accept groundbait and, if they do, a lot of the problems associated with getting your feed down in fast water are ruled out. Bream are the obvious example but other species, particularly roach and dace, will accept it at times. Small, solid balls of groundbait will get down quickly and, as you know that the fish will be on the bottom, you do not have to search through various depths for them.

Before moving on to the types of rods and reels I use for waggler fishing, I will just run through one example of a deep-flowing venue where I have had some success with the waggler in recent times. The River Severn, at Shrewsbury, is the place I have in mind.

Many of the pegs on this stretch are over 10ft (3m) deep and winter rain often gives the water plenty of pace. The target species are roach and dace and most of them insist on feeding on the bottom, well out from the bank. My usual float for them locks with three AAs and has a thickish insert. I usually fish with the bait just tripping the bottom, so I do not need a really thick tip. The shotting down the line, if the river is pacey, will start with three no. 8s closest to the hook and then five or six no. 6s above that. All of the shot are strung out at 9in (24cm) intervals. The target species are not particularly big so I can get away with my $1\frac{1}{2}$lb reel line: and, if the wind is not very severe, the line is treated with flotant, so that I get a good clean strike.

I feed well upstream and watch carefully where the bites come from in relation to my feed. If the bites are at the bottom of the peg then I will also look to catch some fish right at the top of my peg, off the upstream angler's feed. My feeding is kept light, as the target species are ones which can easily be overfed. In mild weather I might use $1\frac{1}{2}$pt, less if it is freezing cold.

I nearly always do well at Shrewsbury with this approach and it works just as well at many other venues.

## RODS

Obviously the rod should be as light as possible. You are going to be holding it for most of the day, and this should not be hard work. The main thing that I look for in a float rod, particularly for waggler fishing, is that it will bend to some extent in the middle section. Often when striking there is a lot of loose line to pick up and a long sweeping strike is required. If I connect with a large powerful fish, which happens to be heading rapidly in the other direction, I want the rod to absorb the shock. Some rods, with a very pronounced tip action, fail to do this: obviously this can lead to 'crack-offs' when light lines are being used.

It goes without saying that the rings need to be of a quality which will not wear out the line, and that the handle should not extend too far below the elbow when you are holding the rod. When rods were heavier, handles were often longer to help counterbalance the weight of the rod, but I fail to see a use for extra-long handles on modern rods. Have a look at the reel fittings as well; some work loose far easier than others and can be very irritating. Metal fittings are also very cold to hold with bare hands in winter. A far as length is concerned, I used 13ft rods for float fishing, though I also carry a 14ft to use in pegs that are just too deep for a 13ft model.

I prefer to use open-faced reels for all of my fishing. Many anglers still like closed-face reels, but I find that the line often needs to be eased off of the reel with your spare hand when running a float through the peg; when doing this there is far less line friction with the open-faced types, so they are best for me. But I am well aware that some very good anglers use closed-face reels, so if you are happy with them there is no need to change.

To finish this chapter, let us have a look at some of the more 'off-standard' uses for a waggler, starting with the use of sliders.

## SLIDING WAGGLER FISHING

If the peg is too deep for a fixed float, and the fish cannot be caught by legering, then sliders come into play (though it should be said that the extra-long 'Bolognase'-type rods which have recently appeared on the market can also be used to overcome extra-deep water).

Fishing a slider is actually very easy, providing you follow a few basic guide-lines:

1.  Make sure that the float carries enough weight to pull the line through the eye of the float.

2.  Ensure the eye at the bottom of the float is small enough to prevent the stop knot from passing through it.

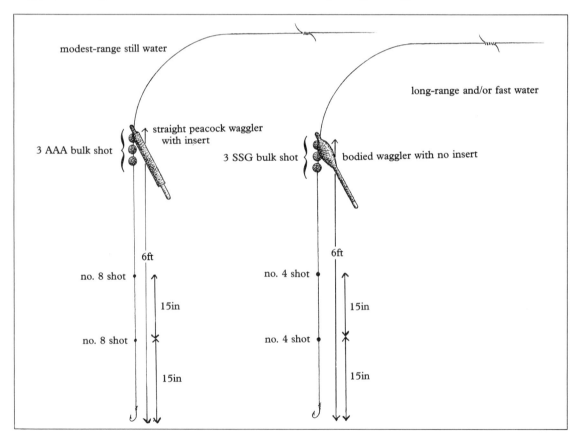

*Typical sliding-float shotting.*

3. Keep the shotting fairly simple to avoid tangles.

The floats I use for slider fishing are simply the larger ones from my normal range; I do not carry separate ones. This includes some with balsa or polystyrene bodies, which rarely get used for fixed waggler fishing. However, the extra weight-carrying capacity is more often of use in a sliding situation.

My shotting is kept very simple. The appropriate bulk shot is attached to the line around 6ft (1.8m) from the hook, below which I will usually use only two shot. They will be closer to the hook than they are to the bulk (to avoid tangles) and their size will depend on the speed of the water being fished: 8s on still water, 6s or 4s on moving water. Typical positioning would be at 15in (38cm) and 30in (76cm) from the hook. The shot also need to be large enough to register lift bites on the float. During the 1993 Drennan super league final, in Ireland, the distance being fished with sliding floats was so great that I ended up using BBs as drop shot, in conjunction with five or six swanshot floats.

I often let the float rest on the bulk shot when casting, but most people prefer to use one small shot well above the bulk for this purpose. This means that the float has less distance to slide and this method can also cast better in windy conditions, which is the main time I adopt it. Another useful idea, which can help to overcome casting problems, is to use a float that has some weight built into its base. This will help the float to keep up with the bulk shot during casting, rather than slide up the line. The stop knot for slider fishing is easy enough to tie after a little practice and I usually tie it with a 3lb or 4lb line.

Finally, here is an extra idea for loosefeeding when fishing deep water. If you start catching fish on the bottom, and they then start to rise up to intercept the feed, it can be worth cutting back the regularity of the feeding: for example, one large pouchful of maggots every four or

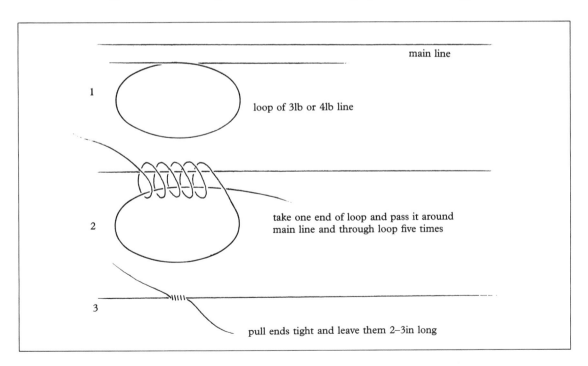

*Sliding float stop knot.*

*This bream fell on the first day of the 1993 Drennan super league final in Ireland.*

*This carp was safely landed on pole tackle in actual fact, showing what can be achieved if the correct elastic is used. However, carp can sometimes be more safely landed on a running line if the angler is not totally aware of what the elastic can do.*

five casts, rather than a few maggots every cast. This change will often keep the fish on the bottom and in very deep water this is preferable, as it can be very difficult to keep track of them if they rise off bottom in 20ft (6m) of water. If you can keep them on the bottom, you will always be fishing at the right depth to catch.

## WAGGLER FISHING FOR CARP

The next off-standard waggler method which deserves a mention is carp fishing. Not the sort which takes place on secret waters, with three rods and a tent, but that enjoyed on the heavily stocked still waters which are springing up all around the country, providing exciting sport for both pleasure and match anglers alike. The

carp in question are often in the 1lb to 5lb range, feed avidly and fight hard.

Catching these fish nearly always requires heavy and constant feeding. The more you feed, the more fish turn up in front of you. Once you have got plenty of fish feeding, large catches are possible – but there is a snag. Decent-sized fish, charging about close to the surface, bump into the line and cause a lot of false bites. Once this starts to happen, the rod needs to be positioned parallel to the bank, where it will cushion the power of a fish which picks up the bait and charges off with it. Continuous use of a catapult will often mean that you have to put the rod into a rest. If the float is constantly darting under, just ignore it and wait for the rod top to go round; striking at false bites will just waste time.

The size of float for this method will, of course, vary with the wind and distance to be fished, but the shotting down the line will be light or non-existent. The bait will be taken close to the surface and, with virtually no weight on the line, the hookbait will be kept on the move by the carp swimming around it. If a strong, heavy hook has to be used because of the size of the fish, it will also be worth considering the use of floating maggots on the hook to counterbalance its weight. To prepare floating maggots, simply put some water in a bait tin with the maggots; they soon take in air and start to float.

This method applies more to summer fishing than winter, because the warmer water makes the fish more active. The same applies to the next method I am going to describe – the 'rhythm' method for dace.

## WAGGLER FISHING FOR SURFACE-FEEDING DACE

This technique used to be particularly deadly on parts of the Warwickshire Avon and Bristol Avon, though a decline in the dace population in recent years has limited its use. However, I am sure that it has uses on other rivers around the country that I am not so familiar with.

It is a method which comes into play when the fish, usually dace, boil on the surface when bait is thrown at them. Getting bites in these circumstances is easy; hitting them is another matter.

The float which I use to catch these fish would usually be in the region of 3 BB to 2½ AA and would be shotted right down, to try to minimize any resistance to a fish taking the bait. Despite the fish feeding on the surface, the float would be set at a depth of 3–4ft (90–120cm), so that the fish does not feel the float the moment it picks up the bait. Shotting down the line usually consists of three or four no. 8s, spread between hook and float. Trial and error has revealed this to be the most effective pattern for me.

To fish using this method the float is cast to the far side of the feed area. The rod is then dropped into a rest and maggots are catapulted out: these should land over a wide area between angler and float, something which can be done by firing them at the water rather than into the

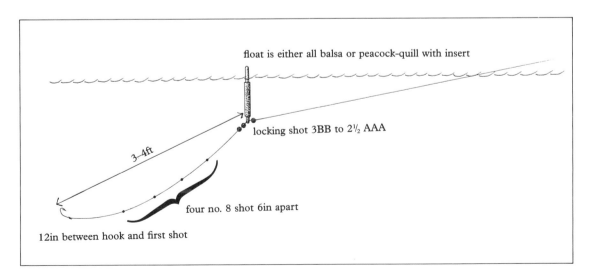

float is either all balsa or peacock-quill with insert

locking shot 3BB to 2½ AAA

3–4ft

four no. 8 shot 6in apart

12in between hook and first shot

*Waggler rig for surface-feeding dace.*

air. By doing this, many will bounce further across the river and the long feed area will be achieved.

The rod is then picked up and a strike is made. If a fish is on, wind it in. If no fish is on, let the float settle again. Early in a session I would feed again at this point, while later in a session I would usually revert to feeding once per cast, when plenty of fish were present. The striking process is repeated until either a fish is hooked or the float is too close to continue, in which case it is, of course, wound in and recast.

Watching the float is usually frustrating and ineffective when dace are feeding in this manner, because the angler's reaction is rarely fast enough to connect. Instead, a counting technique is often the best way to hook the fish. If the maggots are mangled without a fish being hooked, strike at shorter intervals; that is, if

you are striking every ten seconds and failing to hook fish which are chewing the bait, try counting to eight before striking. If this fails, try six seconds, and so on. Eventually, by getting the timing of the strikes right, and giving yourself several chances to catch a fish on each cast, the catch rate will be fast enough to enable big weights to be built up. It all revolves around getting into the right rhythm of casting, feeding and striking.

I should mention that when the dace are feeding in this manner there is rarely any need to fish exceptionally fine. A size 20 hook and $1\frac{1}{2}$lb hooklength would be my normal choice. The line in particular is going to take a lot of stick, and it is not at all unusual to catch large chub in amongst the dace on this method. You might as well give yourself a decent chance of landing them.

# 3  STICKFLOAT AND AVON FLOAT FISHING

A stickfloat is basically a float with two sections; the top of the float will virtually always be made of balsawood, while the base of the float will be made of a much heavier material. Traditionally a heavy cane case is used, but floats are also available with alloy, plastic and wire stems. The final choice is down to personal preference; if it behaves correctly and catches fish for you, use it. (My own preference is for the wire-stemmed versions. I still carry a variety of cane-based floats, but it is extremely rare for these to see action.)

The main reason for the buoyant top and heavy base in these floats is that they are designed to be fished top and bottom on rivers, rather than bottom end only. With silicone tubing holding the float in position at each end, they can be held back to slow the bait down: the reel line is fed out to the float at a slower speed than the current. If a float attached bottom end only is held back it will go under. By holding back the top end of a float, however, it will stay above the surface. The heavy base helps to keep the float upright in the water, rather than lying flat, which could happen with a buoyant base, which always wants to rise to the surface. The heavier base can also help to stabilize the float, making it easier to control in windy conditions.

## USES AND LIMITATIONS

So, when should a stickfloat be used? To start with it will be used close to the near bank, in running water, when a pole is not suitable. Usually this means that the water is quite pacey

*A crucian carp from Willow Park Lakes.*

and the pole is too restrictive when it comes to running the float a long way down the peg.

There will also be times when the size of fish being sought close in will mean that to use the stickfloat, on a running-line rod, will be wiser than using the pole. Fishing for barbel living close to the near bank (like they do on the River Severn) is an excellent example of this situation.

Bankside trees hampering the use of a long pole can also bring the stickfloat into play. It can also be a better method than using the pole in clear water conditions, if the fish can see the pole and are scared by it.

Bigger stickfloats can also be used with devastating effect much further out from the bank, if wind conditions are favourable. Usually that means calm, or a gentle upstream breeze, which will hold the line and therefore the float back, when the line is lifted from the water. This extra float control means that the bait can be slowed down, or lifted from the bottom and allowed to fall again. When this can be achieved the stickfloat can outscore the waggler.

There are also limitations, however, to a stickfloat's use. Strong downstream winds will mean that it can only be fished effectively quite close to the bank. Further out, the line will be blown in front of the float and will then pull the float and bait through the swim at a speed unnatural to the fish. This problem can be eased to some extent by backshotting: putting a small shot 12in (30cm) or 18in (45cm) above the float to sink the line and keep it out of the way of the wind. In stronger winds even this will not make the float fishable.

Powerful upstream winds can also be a nuisance. If the float is too light it will be held back hard by the wind, which is great if that is what the fish want, but not so good if the fish want the bait at a faster speed. Bigger floats or backshotting can help this situation.

Stickfloats also cause problems if the fish are feeding very close to the surface, particularly at ranges which require the use of quite a lot of weight on the line for casting. If the vast majority of the weight has to be situated by the base of the float, it will become very prone to tangles, both when casting and striking. A waggler will usually be better in this situation.

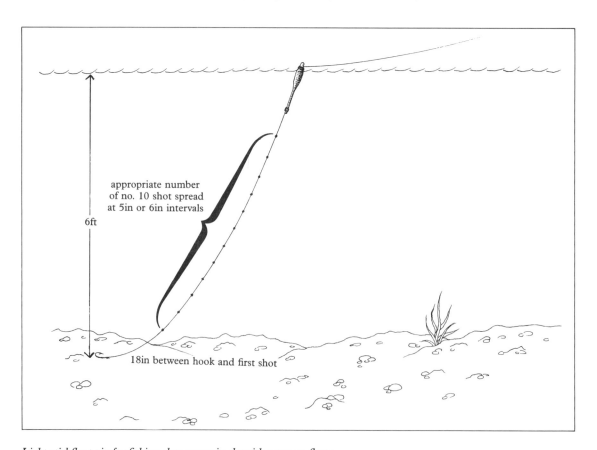

6ft

appropriate number of no. 10 shot spread at 5in or 6in intervals

18in between hook and first shot

*Light stickfloat rig for fishing close range in sluggish summer flows.*

## SIZE AND SHOTTING

I find that the bulk of my stickfloat work is carried out with floats taking five no. 4s upwards. The pole has made many of my smaller sticks all but redundant, though they do occasionally see the light of day, usually because of the reasons I mentioned earlier (overhead trees, fish scared of pole, and so on), so I will still begin with a look at their use.

These floats might only be taking in the region of three no. 6 shot. My main use for these is in sluggish summer rivers, when the fish feed close to near-bank weed-beds. The float will be shotted with a string of small shots: no. 10s in my case, though others go smaller. These shot will be placed on the line at roughly 5in (12cm) or 6in (15cm) intervals, with the closest shot to the hook being about 18in (45cm) away.

This shotting pattern will give a nice slow fall to the bait, particularly when it is near the bottom. Because this method involves fishing at very close range, it is usually wise to cast several yards downstream, to put some distance between angler and fish. When the tackle lands the float is usually held back very hard, so that when the bait lands it stays in one place; this is what the loosefeed will do in the sluggish water this method is generally used in.

My more regularly used range of stickfloats take from five to ten no. 4s. The shotting for these floats is carried out with no. 8 shot. My standard approach is to put three single no. 8s closest to the hook, which are spaced out at 5–6 in (12–15cm) intervals and the one closest to the hook will be about 18 in (45cm) away.

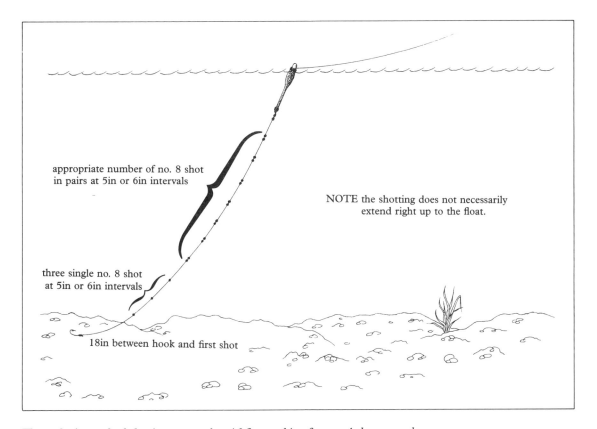

appropriate number of no. 8 shot in pairs at 5in or 6in intervals

NOTE the shotting does not necessarily extend right up to the float.

three single no. 8 shot at 5in or 6in intervals

18in between hook and first shot

*The author's standard shotting pattern for stickfloats taking five no. 4 shot upwards.*

Shotting will continue above these with pairs of no. 8s, at the same intervals. Obviously the bigger floats are likely to be used in deeper water, so there is more room for the shotting to continue up the line.

I find that this shotting system works very well for me. Many anglers prefer to use smaller shot (10s or 12s) close to the hook, but I find that the last 18in (45cm) of unshotted line allows the bait to fall naturally, so I no longer bother with the tiny shot when using these sizes of stickfloat. In very fast water I sometimes have to change from my standard pattern, as the shot required to control the bait cannot be fitted on to the line in no. 8s. In these situations I would simply exchange the no. 8s for no. 6s.

My standard rigs for stickfloat fishing are made up at home and stored on winders. I always carry two ready-made winders for each size of stickfloat, in case of tangles. The floats themselves are not on the winders, but are attached to the main line; the junction knot is then below the float. The reason for keeping the shotting on winders is probably obvious: attaching dozens of no. 8 shot to the line is very time-consuming, particularly if it has to be carried out during a match, following a tangle or similar disaster.

## RODS AND HOOKS

Rods for stickfloat fishing can, if you like, be more tip-actioned than waggler rods, since there will rarely be any need for a long sweeping strike to be cushioned. A stickfloat is nearly always in more direct contact with the rod tip. I still use $1\frac{1}{2}$lb breaking strain main lines when stickfloat fishing. Hooks will vary with baits and size of fish being sought, but will be well balanced to the hook-lengths.

Most of my maggot fishing, on a running line, is carried out with hooks in the range of size 24 to 20. As I write, my most regularly used patterns are Drennan Carbon Casters and Kamasan B520 whisker barbs. These hooks are tied to the extra-fine, co-polymer-type lines. The carbon casters are tied to both 0.07mm diameter and 0.09mm diameter lines, which break at approximately 1lb and $1\frac{1}{2}$lb respectively. These hooks are of reasonably fine wire, yet deceptively strong: I have never had one straighten on a big bonus fish.

If I need a slightly stronger hook and line combination then I swap to the B520s tied to 0.105mm co-polymer line (approximately 2lb breaking strain). These are usually my first choice when chub fishing. For caster fishing the same two patterns see plenty of use, though an 18 or 20 would be my normal size. Hook-length strengths, plus diameters, would remain the same.

These hook and line combinations are all used with my $1\frac{1}{2}$lb main line (remember that standard lines, not co-polymer, nearly always take more strain than advertised, so the main line will still be stronger than the 2lb co-polymer hooklengths!) For stronger hook and line combinations see chapter 8 on feeder fishing, which is where they are more often used.

While on the subject of hooks I should mention that all of mine are tied up at home. If you take your match fishing seriously then I would suggest that this is a wise move. If you tie hooks on the bank it is always tempting to use one which has not come out quite right: you might not be happy with the knot, the line might not be coming away from the spade in the right place, or you may spot some defect with the hook after you have tied it on. If you use it you risk losing fish, if you start again you have wasted time, and if you are not particularly fast at tying hooks to start with, you will already have wasted enough time, even without retying.

By tying at home I can take great care with the quality of the finished product and I am sure this pays off. After all, the hook and hooklength are a vital link between you and any fish you connect with. I would also argue that I can get a pretied hook out of the packet, and attach it to the line, faster than another angler can get a new loose hook out and tie it on.

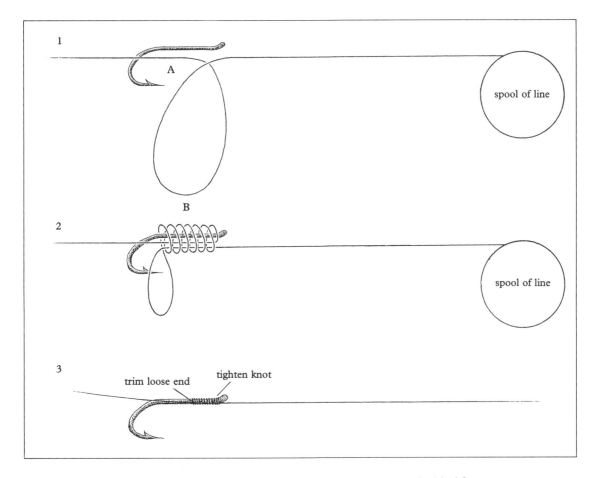

*Whipping knot for use with spade-end hooks: (1) hold the hook and line at point A with right hand, and the large loop of line at point B with left; (2) with your left hand, take the line round the hookshank and line twelve times; (3) To tighten the loop, pull the short loose end with your teeth and the other end by moving the hook away from the line spool, which you can hold in position with your foot. Many people use different methods to tie the same knot. That is fine. If you find an easier way, use it.*

The whipping knot which I use is one in which both ends of the line pass under all of the turns on the hook shank. It might not be the simplest knot to tie, but once learnt it is very reliable. I always tie my hooks with the line coming away from the inside of the spade, and they are all tied to 2½ft (75cm) of line, which is cut to length if I want a shorter hooklength. The hooklength is attached to the main line by the loop-to-loop method, with the loops being made with what I always refer to as the figure-of-eight knot.

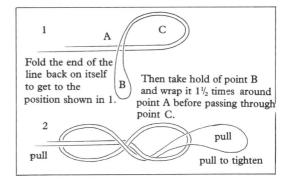

Fold the end of the line back on itself to get to the position shown in 1.

Then take hold of point B and wrap it 1½ times around point A before passing through point C.

*Figure-of-eight loop knot.*

If you lack confidence with the lighter hooklengths, I would suggest running the line through the rod rings and then tying on a 4oz weight. Try lifting it off the ground with the rod and see how much the rod bends: it will probably surprise you. This will help you judge how much pressure you can put on a fish, even with light lines. When a fish breaks you, it is usually for one of three reasons: a) they hit an underwater obstacle, and the shock breaks the line; b) you have tied a weak knot, or damaged the line in some other way, possibly with a shot; or c) the rod is far too stiff and will not absorb the lunges of the fish.

## USING A STICKFLOAT

When using a stickfloat always remember that you are trying to present the bait to the fish in such a way that it cannot be distinguished from the loosefeed, so it must not look suspicious. The classic way to achieve this is to make sure that the hookbait passes through the peg in amongst the loosefeed. If the fish are feeding near the head of the peg, this often means feeding before casting. When the loosefeed has had a couple of seconds to fall, the float is cast out in such a way that the tackle lands in a straight line, with the float at the upstream end and the hook at the downstream. This is usually easiest to achieve with a sideways swing, which starts with the spare hand holding the hook (or the line near it). For longer ranges an overhead cast may be required, but this takes practice, as it is necessary to 'feather' the line as it leaves the reel to avoid tangles. If the tackle lands just downstream of the loosefeed and is then 'held back' hard (that is, little or no line is released from the reel), the bait will fall in front of the float. Once the bait is near the bottom the float can be allowed to run through the swim. If the timing is right the hookbait will fall, and travel through the peg, with the loosefeed.

If the fish are feeding further down the peg it is often best to cast, and then feed. When the float gets to the catching area it is then held back hard, so that the hookbait rises from the bottom and the loosefeed catches up with it. Then the float is released again.

On some days fish will take the bait as it drops, on others they will take it as it runs through the peg. The speed at which it is most readily accepted varies widely and I would recommend running the float through the peg at a range of different speeds and depths until the most productive combination is found. On a river, the ability to slow the float down dramatically is one of the main advantages of using a float attached by both ends.

The fish are most likely to accept the bait while it is dropping, or moving swiftly through the peg, if the water is on the clear side. As the water becomes more coloured the fish have difficulty in seeing the bait and are far more likely to grub around on the bottom to find it. When this happens the most successful method of presenting the bait often involves fishing as far over depth as possible; then inching the float through the peg, so that the hookbait trundles along the bottom very slowly. This is still a natural way of presenting the bait as loosefeed which reaches bottom will also stop, or at least slow down dramatically, as it moves through the swim.

The most frustrating aspect of fishing this way, well over depth, is the snag problems which are often encountered. In coloured water this method will often be used close to the bank, which is the most likely place for bankside trees to have dropped their branches. It pays to try running the float through the peg a few times before the start, in order to establish where the bottom is clear. When you do hook snags make a mental note of their position and try to feed in such a way that you do not have to fish in them.

## AVON FLOAT FISHING

Like stickfloats, Avons are floats which are designed for use in running water and are attached to the line by both ends. However

*A quality roach which fell to maggot.*

they tend to be used in a different manner and usually carry a lot more weight. The Avon floats which I carry start at 6 BB and go up to 12 BB.

My floats are made with balsawood bodies and crow-quill stems, though other materials can be used for both parts of the float; expanded polystyrene in particular, is often used as a body material.

The shotting for these floats tends to be fairly standard and simple. I usually bulk shot the floats 3ft (90cm) from the hook and then place a dropper shot about 12in (30cm) from the hook, usually a no. 6. Sometimes this will be replaced by two no. 8s, positioned slightly apart, to give a slower fall to the bait. If the float being used changes to a larger or smaller one, the size of the bulk shotting is usually the only difference. This bulk shotting is usually carried out with AB shot.

This shotting pattern gives a very smooth presentation of the bait, usually down near the bottom, which can be deadly for skimmers and

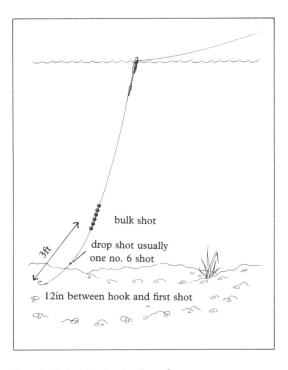

*Standard shotting for the Avon float.*

sometimes bigger bream; it can also be best for roach at times. Despite the size of the floats being used, they are surprisingly sensitive and can be used for small fish.

These floats are at their best in an upstream breeze, and can still be used effectively in strong upstream winds, when the larger sizes will come into play. The heavy bulk shot will pick up any flow and pull the lightweight float behind in a very efficient manner difficult to achieve with a float carrying less shot.

The lower stretches of the Bristol Avon are classic venues for the Avon float. The predominant south-west wind blows upstream and, if fishing at range, the deep sluggish summertime water is often best tackled with a heavily shotted Avon, rather than a more lightly shotted stickfloat, which would sometimes struggle to move down the peg against the wind.

If the fish were feeding on the drop or well off bottom, at range, then the waggler would still be my first choice. But if the fish are on the bottom and wind conditions are appropriate, then the Avon can be a winner.

I tend to use these floats in comparatively deep water. But the smaller 6 BB floats sometimes come out in only 4–5ft (1.2–1.5m) of water, when bleak or other tiny surface-feeding fish are grabbing the bait on its way down. The shot can then be further moved down the line, until the bait is being taken down to the bottom quickly enough to avoid the nuisance fish.

Another situation where these floats can be particularly useful is where excess tree growth makes overhead, or even sideways, casting out of the question. A decent-size Avon float can be cast surprisingly long distances with an underarm swing. The float is lightweight enough to obediently follow the bulk shot. Wagglers can also be cast in this manner but distance is more difficult to achieve and tangles are more common.

Because of the type of presentation being achieved and the species which appreciate it, groundbait is often used in conjunction with the Avon float. Light regular loosefeed can often persuade fish to move off bottom. Small, hard balls of groundbait, loaded with feed (often casters) will usually attract and hold the fish species being sought, in the place where they are easiest to catch with an Avon. Alternatively, large pouchfuls of loosefeed at irregular intervals can also keep the fish well down in the water, if they are scared of groundbait.

I cannot conclude this chapter without mentioning a type of float that quite a few anglers use instead of Avons, and which I occasionally use in particularly fast water, when its extra buoyancy at the tip can be helpful. I am talking about balsas which, as their name suggests, are made from balsawood, usually in a cigar-like shape. If I decide to use these floats in powerful flows, I bulk shot them in the same way as an Avon, but tend to use slightly more weight below the bulk to keep the bait down. This shotting would usually involve three or four no. 6s rather than the single no. 6 more often used with the Avon.

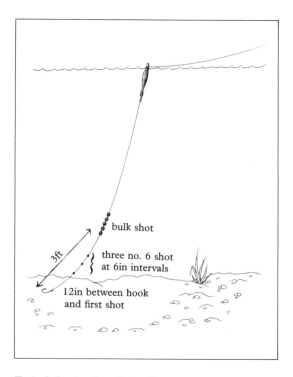

*Typical shotting for a balsa float.*

# 4 POLES AND ELASTIC SET-UPS

## CHOOSING A POLE

To start with I will repeat something that has been written many times before, but which is certainly worth restating: always go for the longest pole you can afford. From a pleasure fishing point of view this does not really matter, but in a match angling situation it eventually will. If you buy an 8m pole you will soon find yourself in situations where 10m or 11m would be far better. Far banks of canals are a prime example: few can be reached with 8m, but an extra 2–3m would bring them within range. The same can often apply in other waters,

where you might struggle to reach the depth of water which you need to fish in. If you intend to do quite a lot of match fishing a decent pole is a very worthwhile investment.

When you are actually choosing a pole there are several important points to watch for. To start with, check on the availability of spare sections. No matter how careful you are, you will eventually break a section (or, more likely, have someone else do it for you as they pass by), or drop one into the water. If spare sections cannot be obtained the whole pole becomes useless, so check with your local tackle dealer before buying; he should be well aware which companies offer a good, quick spares service.

*Alan Scotthorne gently slides his pole back to bring in another roach.*

Another feature worth looking for is that the sections slide smoothly apart. If they stick badly this is likely to slow you down severely when breaking down the pole to land a fish. This problem is usually reasonably easy to correct by some gentle sanding with very fine paper, but make sure that it can be eliminated before parting with your money.

The next point to consider concerns the strength of tackle which you intend to use with the pole. If you intend to use it in conjunction with heavy tackle, to go after carp or other powerful fish, make sure that the pole is strong enough for the job. Some of the very light-weight poles are excellent for standard fishing with light lines, but would be in danger of breaking under the strain of fighting big fish on strong lines. The same concern over strength also applies if you intend to use the pole for fishing to hand, without elastic, on the huge-weight venues found in Ireland or Scandinavia. Swinging in a one-pound-plus fish is not a job that all poles can handle. Some poles are so thin-walled that they will flex quite consider-ably under finger pressure. Again the tackle dealer should be able to advise you on which poles are strongest if you do intend to use heavy tackle.

Having pointed out the limitations of some very lightweight poles, I am now going to add that lightness is a very desirable quality in a long pole which is being used for the more normal English fishing with light lines. As poles become longer, the need for lightness increases: 12–14m, or longer, is quite a handful if used in windy conditions for a full five-hour match. Lightness at these lengths will certainly become a very important consideration. I actually carry two long poles with me: one for normal, light line work and a second slightly heavier, but far stronger pole for heavy-duty use.

Stiffness is also important. The ideal pole for use with elastic would be completely rigid. That is not possible, but get as close as you can to that ideal. A pole which bends and wob-bles all over the place in windy conditions will make tackle control very difficult. Striking

*A pole-caught carp makes its last surge before giving up.*

will also be badly affected by a floppy pole, as there will be a delayed reaction, rather than a crisp and immediate connection with the biting fish. Incidentally, many poles, particularly towards the cheaper end of the market, tend to be very usable when the butt section is removed, but far more cumbersome at their full length. Make sure that you have handled the pole at its full length before buying.

Poles also come in both 'put-in' and 'put-over' designs. Put-in means that the tip section slides inside the second section to join them together, and the second section then slides inside the third, and so on. With the put-over type the tip section slides over the top of the second section, and so on down the pole. Both types work perfectly well, but joint wear can be more serious on the put-in type, and in excessive cases a section can slide straight through the one which it is meant to join with. To avoid this, keep the joints clean and free from the dirt and grit which will gradually wear them down; you should then be safe from any problems. With put-over type poles, joint wear will simply lead to the male joint sliding slightly further inside the female, which does not cause any problems.

I use poles of both types and always clean the joints off with a towel before assembling them: as well as avoiding wear, this encourages the sections to slide smoothly apart when breaking the pole down.

## ELASTICS AND ELASTIC FITTINGS

Let us move on now to discuss the elastic set-ups for use with a long pole. To start with, the pole tip needs to be fitted with a self-lubricating PTFE bush, but before you start to fit one think carefully. It is easy to get carried away with cutting back the pole tip to make a bush fit until you suddenly realize that you are losing quite a lot of length. This is of particular concern if you are fitting a bush to take strong, thick elastic.

For pole tips which will be used with thick elastic I always fit an external bush; this saves cutting back quite a lot of pole tip when compared to an internal version, which will take up a good deal of the space that the elastic needs to pass through. For thinner elastics I still use internal bushes.

For any readers who do not understand why PTFE bushes are used, I should point out that their function is to prevent friction between the elastic and the pole tip when playing a fish. Friction would eventually damage the elastic and also hinder its smooth passage into and out of the pole.

When it comes to pole elastics, the lengths used vary widely from angler to angler. I put mine through two sections, which means about 4ft (1.2m) on my main pole (5ft/1.5m in the case of the stronger pole which I carry for heavy duty fishing). Until quite recently I used 2½ ft (75cm) but swopped to 4ft (1.2m) because I found it to be safer when dealing with large bonus fish – there was far less chance of the elastic 'bottoming out' and the fish breaking the line.

To attach the elastic inside the poles I normally use uni-bungs. These can be cut down to fit inside virtually any pole but I will offer a word of advice: do not cut much off the centre cord. If the bung slides further up the pole while you are playing a big fish, and takes the end of the cord with it, you are going to have a problem getting it back out. It is far better to leave it long to start with.

At the tip end of the elastic I currently use the readily available stonfo connectors, though I do doctor them slightly. I discard the external slide-on parts and replace them with silicone tubing, which I find smoother and therefore more tangle-proof.

To stretch in and out of the pole tip smoothly, the elastic needs to be lubricated. There are many commercial varieties of lubri-

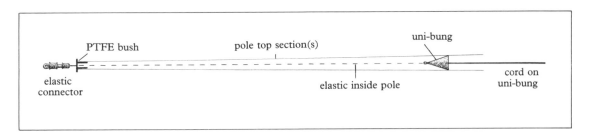

*Internal elastic set-up for poles.*

cant available, but I use washing-up liquid thinned down with water, which works perfectly well for me! If, when lubricated, the elastic does not retract back into the pole properly, simply shorten one end of it. Once you have got the length right, always make sure that you replace it with the same length when it wears out, to avoid repeating the problem.

Replacing your elastics several times during a season is a very wise move. Always keep a close eye on them, as they will eventually perish. This applies particularly during the summer months, when long exposure to strong sunlight appears, in my experience, to cause deterioration. It is far better to replace the elastic than wait for a fish to break it.

I also keep a close eye on the knot where the elastic joins the uni-bung; this area does not perish in my experience, but the effect of the lubricant on the knot can cause it to work loose. I have only been caught out by this problem once, but it cost me a lot of money, so I always check the knot when tackling up. I also leave the loose end quite long to help avoid a disaster.

Elastic strengths will obviously vary with the size of the fish being sought, but I do not find the really fine elastics, no. 1 or no. 2, useful: the finest which I use is no. 3. I am not convinced that the really light ones set the hook properly – though this probably would not apply to anglers who use much shorter lengths of elastic which will come closer to bottoming out on the strike; this puts more pressure on the hook to pull it into the fish. No. 3 and no. 4 elastics cover most of my fishing, but no. 5 and no. 7 also see some action during the course of a season when bigger fish are around.

Keep an eye on elastic diameters. When buying, I have found considerable variation, and I suspect that some have been accidentally mislabelled. If in doubt compare them closely to the old ones you are changing.

To fit new elastics in the pole you will need a wire threader. I use the type which has a diamond-shaped eye at one end to grip the end of the elastic. When replacing elastic I first attach the stonfo connector to one end; then I cut the elastic to the correct length and attach it to the wire threader. Once I have threaded it through the appropriate pole sections, I tie a loop in the end of it to enable me to attach it to the uni-bung.

# 5 LONG POLE FISHING WITHOUT BLOODWORMS

When choosing pole floats, body shape is probably the most important factor; I tend to avoid floats with very long, slim bodies. They do not usually behave well when held back in rivers (polesticks, with their heavy stems, are an exception to this rule). I prefer floats with comparatively wide bodies, normally round or rugby-ball shapes. On still waters inverted pear shapes also see a lot of use, as they do not need to be held back and the body shape is very stable.

Tip materials need to be varied from very fine tips, often of wire, for use when fishing off bottom, to much thicker tips, usually of plastic or fibreglass, which can be seen at distance and are also more practical for fishing over depth; in such a situation a wire tip would probably continually drag under.

A quick check with a micrometer has revealed that the wire used in my wire-tipped floats is 0.4mm in diameter, though when painted this increases to just over 0.6mm. At the other end of the scale, the floats which I use for fishing over depth, at range, have tips which are close to 1.5mm thick. My most frequently used floats would fall in between these two extremes and incorporate tips of just over 1mm in diameter.

The choice of materials used for float stems is largely down to personal preference. Wire seems to be the most stable material, but the same-sized float body with a cane stem will take more weight further down the line, which will also help provide stability. I carry floats with wire, cane, carbon fibre and fibreglass stems – and they all work well. My floats are always attached to the line with two pieces of silicone tubing on the stem, to prevent slipping.

## PREPARING FOR A MATCH

I cannot over-stress the importance of plumbing the depth carefully before you commence pole fishing. It is vital to have a mental picture of the contours of the bottom of your peg. Also I always mark the depth on the pole, with correcting fluid or marker pen, so that I can always reset the float to the correct depth after moving it for any reason. It is usually necessary to mark several depths on the pole if you are fishing up and down a shelf. The loosefeed will not all land in one spot, so you will often need to vary the distance at which you are fishing; this frequently means a change in depth as well.

If I am not absolutely certain which type of rig will be used, I will set up all possibilities. If my first choice fails, all I have to do is pick up another one.

A lot of thought should also go into the positioning of your nets, bait, spare tackle, and so on, before the match starts. To fish a long pole properly you have to be seated and it is important, in a match situation, that you can reach everything without getting up. Efficiency is a key factor. I will use my own layout as an example.

The keepnet is positioned in front of me, towards the left-hand side, with its mouth parallel to the water. I am right-handed, so the fish will be swung into my left hand: the net is positioned underneath the catching position so that any fish which drop off will fall straight into it. The landing net is also placed close to my left-hand side, in such a way that I can pick it up without looking for it. Hookbaits are kept

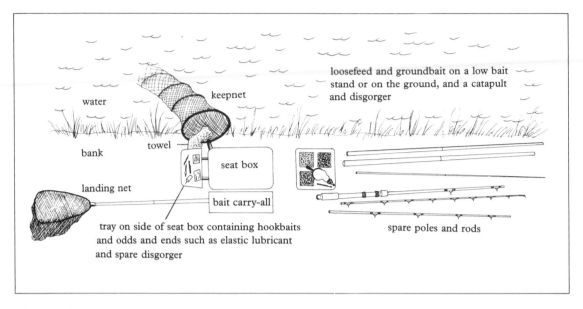

*The author's tackle layout when sitting down.*

in a tray attached to the left-hand side of the seat box. When rebaiting I hold the hook in my right hand and the bait with my left, so the left-hand side is the best place for hookbait. The tray is also home to some spare pole elastic lubricant. Finally, I keep a towel on the left-hand side, usually draped over the side of the keepnet mouth. If the rebaiting hand becomes too slimy, it can then be easily wiped.

On the right-hand side of my box you will find loosefeed, groundbait and a catapult. When I use a catapult, it is natural for me to hold the catapult with my left hand and pull back the pouch with my right. So it is the right hand which also fills the pouch and, consequently, the loosefeed needs to be on my right-hand side. This also fits in well with my method of holding the pole while feeding. The butt of the pole is on my right-hand side and I sit turned slightly to the right so that the pole goes across my legs for additional support. When I want to feed, I fold my body over the pole so that the butt is held between my stomach and legs. This leaves me with both hands free to use a catapult.

Because I am bending over a long way the loosefeed and catapult are either placed on the ground or on a low bait stand. Groundbait, for long pole fishing, is usually thrown in with the right hand. As soon as the terminal tackle is laid out on the water, I hold the pole butt across my legs by pushing down on it with my left hand, leaving my right hand free to pick up and throw the groundbait.

A disgorger is also placed on my right-hand side, with a second one at the top of my bait apron, if I am wearing it. My hookwallet is usually immediately behind me, in my bait/netbag. If there is water behind me (in other words, if I am sitting out from the bank) then the hookwallet will be found in a drawer of my seat box.

One final piece of preparation needs to be undertaken before the start of a long session on the pole: make sure that you have worked out where to feed the pole back. Sometimes you will have a convenient grass bank to slide it over, or maybe a tree branch in a hedge; but more likely you will need to put up a pole roller or position your rod holdall in a suitable place to feed the pole over. You need to be able to feed the pole in and out smoothly and quickly,

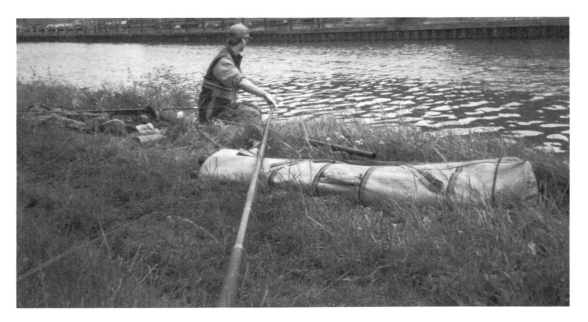

*Preparing to break down the pole to land what is obviously a good fish from the Gloucester Canal.*

without hitting any obstacles. Thick hedgerows could be your worst enemy!

If I stand in the water, fishing a running line, the layout remains similar. The nets are in identical position on the left, the hookbait is transferred to a bait apron, and on the right-hand side the bait stand doubles as a back rod rest, and a front rod rest is added. (The rod is dropped while feeding by catapult.)

If I am float fishing with a running line sitting down, I do not bother with a rod rest. I either hold the rod between my knees or sit on the handle.

You do not have to copy my positioning of the various items of equipment, but you do need to work out a layout which suits you. Efficiency saves time which can be used to catch more fish – very desirable from a match fishing point of view.

Once you have got the right rigs tackled up, you have carefully plumbed the depth and your equipment is thoughtfully laid out, you are ready to move on to the actual feeding and fishing.

*The author concentrates very hard at the start of a match; here he is preparing to throw a ball of groundbait.*

## POLE FISHING IN STILL WATERS

### Shallow-Water Fishing with Squatts and Pinkies

I most commonly use the smaller sizes of pole float for squatt and pinkie fishing on canals. The majority of fish in these venues are usually caught well over towards the far side, where there is less disturbance from anglers and other towpath users. The security provided by cover is an added attraction of the far bank on many canals.

The fish will generally be found at various points, up and down the far shelf. The colour of the water is usually the main guide to their whereabouts: if the canal is highly coloured the fish tend to move closer to the banks, but as the water clears the fish will normally retreat to the security of the deeper water.

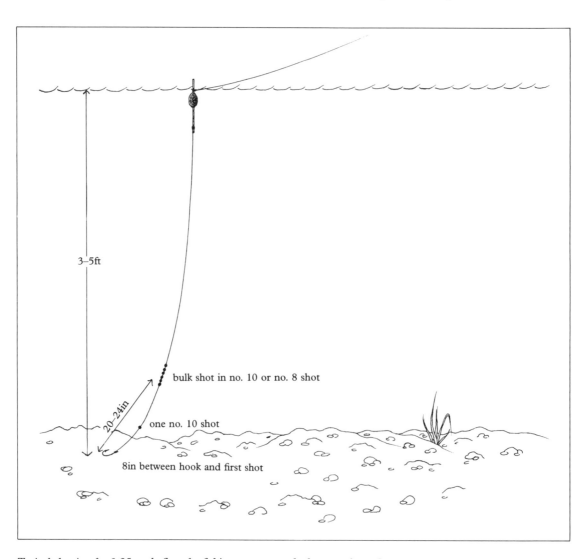

3–5ft

bulk shot in no. 10 or no. 8 shot

20–24in

one no. 10 shot

8in between hook and first shot

*Typical shotting for 0.25g pole float for fishing on or near the bottom of canals.*

There are two main shotting patterns which I use to catch these fish. The first one is designed to catch them on the bottom. The float will be shotted with bulk shot (no. 10s or no. 8s) at a distance of 20–24in (50–60cm) from the hook, while below the bulk there will be just one or two no. 10 shot, positioned about 8in (20cm) from the hook.

This rig is at its most effective when the venue is highly coloured and the fish have to grub around on the bottom for food, because they cannot see it falling through the water. The float which sees most use when I fish like this takes 0.25g, and would typically be used in 3–5ft (0.9–1.5m) of water. Obviously float size would be stepped up for deeper water or adverse wind conditions, but the shotting pattern would remain the same.

As the water becomes clearer the fish are far more likely to grab a falling bait, so the shotting

changes to take this into account. The bulk shot, used to take the bait swiftly to the bottom is replaced with a string of small shot. These shot will be a mixture of no. 10s and no. 13s, with the 13s closest to the hook. The exact positioning varies quite widely; sometimes they will be strung out over a large area, on other occasions they will all be one or two inches apart on the bottom half of the line. It pays to experiment until the most successful pattern on the day emerges. I should also mention that my closest shot to the hook when fishing this rig will be 12in (30cm) away. Most anglers would use style leads for this type of fishing, but I am quite happy that I can achieve the desired effect by sticking to the tiny sizes of shot. It seems to work for me!

The float which I use will also differ from the one used for fishing on the bottom. It will incorporate a finer tip, as I do not have to worry

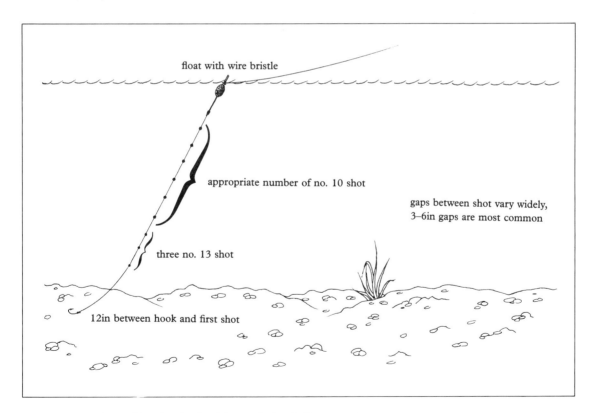

float with wire bristle

appropriate number of no. 10 shot

gaps between shot vary widely, 3–6in gaps are most common

three no. 13 shot

12in between hook and first shot

*Typical shotting for catching 'on the drop' in canals (or similar venues).*

about it dragging under, and is likely to have a wire stem, particularly in shallow water, as I do not want too much weight further down the line.

The hooks used in both of these rigs for squatt and pinkie fishing, are usually very fine wire size 24s tied to co-polymer lines of 1lb breaking strain (0.07mm diameter) or lighter (0.05mm or 0.06mm). The stronger line would be used in more coloured water, where there is more chance of hooking large fish and also less chance of fish seeing the line. For the main lines on these rigs I sometimes still use a standard 1lb breaking-strain line, although I am now changing over to the co-polymers, which do an excellent job provided that the shot are attached to the line with great care.

The main target species for this method is often small roach, and to help hold them in the peg, hemp seed can be very helpful, especially in the summer months when its weight will keep it in place despite the wash of the boat traffic. I usually put in a couple of pouchfuls to start with, then top up at irregular intervals: particularly after boats have passed. Groundbait can also be useful to get fish into the peg and hold them there, though I would tend to shy away from it in very clear water. With both groundbait and hemp seed I suspect that the smell is important in attracting fish.

In addition to hemp and groundbait I also feed squatts. These are fed at regular intervals; in the summer I would expect to use up to a pint of them, in the winter far less – maybe only a quarter of a pint. When this method was first used far greater quantities were introduced, with anglers successfully feeding 3–4 pints. This really heavy feeding seems to have lost its effect on hard-fished venues, but if you fish suitable waters which have not been exposed to heavy squatt feeding, try it out.

With squatts being catapulted in at regular intervals the fish should soon find them and, because squatts sink so slowly, are likely to start moving off bottom to intercept them, especially in clearer water. When this happens the strung shot rig will probably attract most bites, but do not ignore the bulk-shotted float. Bigger fish in the form of better roach and skimmers will often stay on the bottom underneath the more active youngsters.

The main reason for using a long pole, instead of a running line, at a range which you could easily cast to is to take advantage of the perfect float control which the pole offers. The terminal tackle can be placed in exactly the right spot every time and then be allowed to move with the flow, held dead still, eased through the peg at any desired speed, or lifted to allow the bait to fall again.

The most effective presentation will vary from day to day and from venue to venue, so if you are not catching, start experimenting. I have just listed plenty of possibilities, and do not forget to try further up or down the shelf (if you are on a canal) as well.

The best float control can be achieved with a fairly short length of line between pole tip and float, about 2ft (60cm). But in calm conditions it is often possible to get away with a longer line. This is because you will not have to feed the pole back so far before breaking it down to land the fish, so over five hours the time saved will yield a few extra fish.

In extremely windy conditions too short a line can lead to the pole tip pulling at the float as it is blown around. The best way to overcome this is to lengthen the line and add a shot (a no. 8 will usually be sufficient) half-way between pole tip and float. The movement of the pole tip will then be absorbed by the shot and the float should be controllable again.

Hookbaits should also be varied when feeding squatts. A single large squatt is usually the best bait for consistent catching, but double squatts or a single pinkie can often be best for slightly bigger fish, particularly skimmers. As well as being very effective up and down the far shelves of canals, this method also works well on lakes, slow-moving drains, and also at much shorter ranges on canals where the nearside fish demand perfect bait presentation.

*The elastic does its job on another powerful fish.*

## Angling for Larger Fish

The same shotting patterns and floats can also be used to catch larger fish from canals, or similar-depth venues, by fishing them with big maggots or casters. On many canals light feeding with these baits will attract quality roach, better skimmers and other decent fish. Often these fish will stay in the deep channel towards the centre of the canal and will fall for a single maggot or caster which is held completely still on the bottom.

For maggot fishing I would use a size 24 or 22 hook, but change to a slightly stronger pattern than used for squatts. Casters would usually be fished on a size 20. The hooklengths should generally be 1lb breaking strain, co-polymer types; if the expected fish included anything particularly powerful, however, I would step up the line strength. The pole elastic for better fish is also likely to be increased from the no. 3, which I would use for squatt fishing, to no. 4. The need to keep the bait still would also mean that if the water was flowing to any extent, a slightly larger float might be required. When fishing for bigger fish I would

also cut out the hemp from my feeding, and groundbait as well, if quality roach were the main target.

Another area on canals which throws up quality fish is the shallow water tight to the far bank. Overhanging trees or bushes usually provide a home for decent fish, as do reed-beds. Far banks which have been piled are also worth some attention, as the piles will have prevented the bank from collapsing, so the water next to the piles will be comparatively deep. The depth gives the fish added security. If the water is exceptionally deep then the same rigs which I have just described for fishing down the shelves will be suitable. But for fishing in very shallow water different rigs will be required.

The floats which are effective in shallow water at the far bank are usually fished over depth, to keep the bait still, and often have one or more shot lying on the bottom to act as an anchor which will hold the float and bait in position. This applies particularly when fishing under awkward, overhanging bushes: then the tackle should be carefully placed in position and the pole tip retracted so that a strike can be made without hitting bushes with the pole.

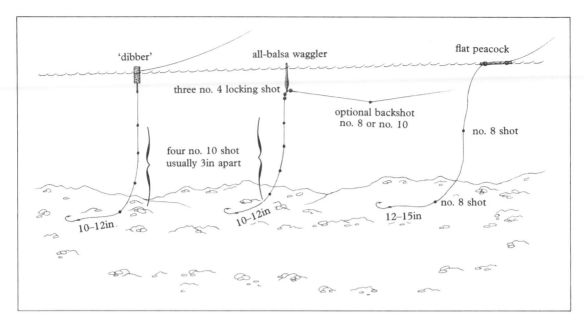

*The author's three rig variations for fishing shallow canal far banks.*

As the pole tip will not be above the float, an anchoring shot often becomes essential to hold it in position.

There are three types of float which I would consider for shallow, far-bank use. The first of these is usually known as a 'dibber' and consists of a short balsa or peacock-quill body and a short wire stem. Often these floats are bristleless, as a bristle would drag under too easily; instead they are fished with just the top of the balsa or peacock quill showing. They are fished top and bottom and what little shot they take would be spread out – usually three or four no. 10s or possibly no. 8s.

Sometimes, in very strong winds, small top-and-bottom floats become uncontrollable. In this situation I would swap to a short, all-balsa, bottom-end-only waggler. Typically this would be locked on the line with three no. 4 shot and would take three no. 10s or no. 8s down the line. If necessary a backshot would be used to keep the line out of the way of the wind.

The final float worth mentioning is rather off-standard, but in very shallow water, where the fish can see the float and are scared, it

becomes a winner. It consists of a 1in (2.5cm) piece of unpainted peacock quill attached to the line by silicone tubing. I shot it with just two no. 8 shot, at least one of which will be on the bottom to anchor it in position. The float will lie flat on the surface, held in position by the shot, and will register bites by running across the surface as a fish moves off with the bait. I know it sounds unlikely, but if fish are frightened by normal floats, it really does work.

## Fishing in Deep Water

Pole fishing in much deeper water is something which I have some experience of, as I have fished the Gloucester Canal many times over the years, and that definitely comes under the heading of deep. The methods I learnt while fishing the Gloucester, have worked equally well for me on other still or very slow-moving venues around the country, so they should also work well for other anglers.

### Fishing on the Bottom
When fishing for decent-size fish, on or near

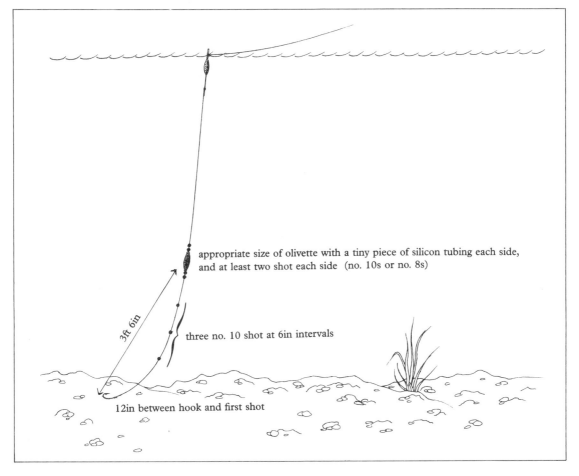

appropriate size of olivette with a tiny piece of silicon tubing each side, and at least two shot each side (no. 10s or no. 8s)

3ft 6in

three no. 10 shot at 6in intervals

12in between hook and first shot

*The author's standard shotting pattern for pole fishing in still or slow-moving water.*

the bottom, I tend to stick to one basic shotting pattern. This consists of an olivette around 3½–4ft (105–120cm) from the hook and then three no. 10 shot below it. The closest shot to the hook will usually be at least 12in (30cm) away and the other two no. 10s will be at 6in (15cm) intervals above it. This shotting pattern will get the bait well down in the water quickly, but then the hookbait falls slowly through the last few feet of water; this allows fish to be caught on the drop as well as on the bottom.

I use olivettes instead of a bulk of small shot once I get to float sizes of 0.5g or more, because the numbers of small shot involved start to get out of hand. I keep the olivettes in position

with at least two tiny shot each side of them, and to stop the shot being moved by the olivette under the pressure of striking, I slide two tiny pieces of very thin silicone tubing on to the line, one on each side of the olivette, to act as a buffer between olivette and shot.

Size of float used will vary with depth. For example: 1g for 10ft (3m) of water would be about right, dropping to around 0.6g or 0.75g for 8ft (2.4m) of depth, and increasing to 1.5g for 14ft (4.2m). No. 4 elastic would be my normal choice for this type of fishing and hooks would be on the fine side of medium wire: currently I use Kamasan B511s if I am fishing 0.07 hooklengths or Drennan Carbon

Casters if I am fishing 0.09 hooklengths. Once I get up to 1.5g floats, or bigger, I would also tend to increase the main line strength from 1lb to 1½lb (standard lines),. or 2lb or more (co-polymers).

If bream, of any size, are the main target species, it is usually possible to feed groundbait. Casters, squatts or possibly both, should be added to the mix, and by feeding fairly hard balls of bait the fish will usually be kept on the bottom. I would generally start a session by feeding between two and six orange-sized balls of groundbait and then top up with smaller, egg-sized balls. On some days these balls will not worry the fish and they can be introduced at regular intervals; on other days the fish tend to back off for a while when you feed, so if this happens do not feed while you are catching.

If you are feeding squatts in groundbait, and catching decent bream, do not ignore the squatts as a possible hookbait. You might be surprised at just how many sizeable bream fall for a bunch of squatts.

If decent roach are your deep-water pole fishing target, you are likely to be back to loose-feeding. Sometimes they will move well off bottom to intercept the loosefeed – I will explain how to tackle that later. For now just assume that they stay on the bottom.

The first point to remember with roach is that they are often found closer in than bream; bream fishing is usually carried out at quite long range as they show their fondness of deep water. Roach are different, often moving into the base of any ledges which are present. Bear this in mind when deciding where to fish, so that you do not go past the fish. The terminal tackle will not show any real changes. I use size 24 or 22 hooks for maggots and size 20s or 18s for casters, though they will rarely be tied to anything except 0.07 diameter hooklengths.

The quantity of loosefeed will vary widely, depending largely on the head of fish present. But do not forget to work the hookbait around the whole area where the loosefeed is landing, rather than just putting it in exactly the same spot every time.

*More pole fishing action from Ireland.*

If you need to fish for very small roach, or other tiny fish, in deep water, the shotting will need to change to something very similar to the set-up I described for squatt fishing on shallower venues (the olivette will move to within 2ft/60cm of the hook, and one or two droppers will be about 8in/20cm from the hook). In low-weight winter matches, where bloodworms are banned, this method can sometimes be a winner if fished with squatts and pinkies. It rarely wins in summer because: a) quality fish tend to dominate deeper venues in summer, especially when bloodworms are banned, and b) most tiny fish prefer shallower water in summer!

### Fishing off the Bottom

When fish move well off bottom to feed you need different techniques to tackle the situation. Here is an example. Worsborough Reservoir, just outside Barnsley, is a venue where the fish feed well off bottom during hot summer months; not only roach, but bream, are particularly enthusiastic shallow feeders.

The rig which I use here will be 0.25g or less and will be shotted with small shot strung out. The closest shot to the hook would be three no. 13s, and above these would be the required number of no. 10s. The closest shot to the hook would start at a distance of about 18in (45cm); the other shot would be strung out above this at 4in (10cm) or 5in (12cm) intervals. Some of the no. 10s closest to the float might need to be in pairs to fit them all on the line. The usual starting depth for this method is 5–6ft (1.5–1.8m) at Worsborough.

This shotting pattern is quite similar to the one used for waggler fishing on the drop. The pole rig, however, is better in several ways. To start with, the sensitivity of the bristle on the float means that no. 13s will register on it, so they can safely be used to give the bait a very slow fall. On top of this, the float used will be smaller than a waggler used to cast to the same spot; furthermore the pole offers far more control to the float once it is in the water, including a more direct strike.

The 18in (45cm) distance between hook and first shot is designed to give an even slower drop to the bait. In my experience this length will work well when quality fish are the target, as they virtually always move off far enough with the bait in their mouths to show a bite. When I am after tiny fish this distance is shortened dramatically, as they have a tendency to suck the bait and reject it without moving far enough to register a bite on the float.

The best feeding pattern to keep the bream high up in the water involves groundbait mixed very wet for maximum cloud effect. A small ball of this should be fed every time the tackle is laid on the water; at the same time feed squatts and casters by catapult. By feeding this mixture of bait, some of it will be falling past the fish at nearly all times, since squatts, casters and groundbait all sink at different speeds.

Bites on this method can come very quickly, so the organization discussed earlier in the chapter will be vital. If you do become efficient at this style, huge catches are possible. I can vividly remember a practice session at Worsborough where I caught something in the region

*Action from the Gloucester Canal. Note how the pole is held by the knees so that both hands are free to unhook the fish.*

of sixty bream on the pole. It was a particularly educational day as, once the bream had arrived in numbers, I could dictate where they fed. The soft groundbait and loosefeed would bring them high up in the water, but if I swapped to small hard balls and cut out the loosefeed, I could take them down to the bottom of the 11ft (3.3m)-deep swim and catch them there with a much heavier olivette rig.

Exactly the same pole rig as for catching the bream well off bottom could be used for decent roach feeding in the same manner. With decent roach, however, loosefed maggots or casters are nearly always better than groundbait. Try feeding two or three times every cast to keep a constant fall of bait through the water.

## POLE FISHING IN FLOWING WATER

If I am in a situation where I need to get the bait quickly through bleak, tiny dace or other nuisance fish, I am likely to use an olivette rig with three drop shot below it, as I described for fishing deep still waters. But my most commonly used set-ups, for maggot or caster fishing on rivers, are fished with a string of shot just like a stickfloat. Indeed, I am now using polesticks for this kind of work as well as the more traditional pole floats. If the fish stay close enough to be within pole range this method will usually outscore the running-line stickfloat

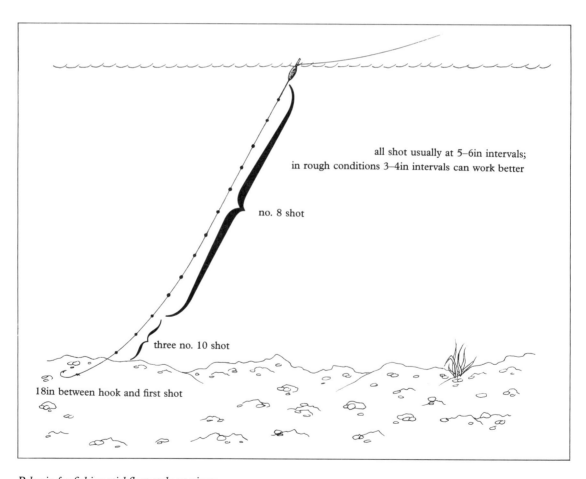

all shot usually at 5–6in intervals;
in rough conditions 3–4in intervals can work better

no. 8 shot

three no. 10 shot

18in between hook and first shot

*Pole rig for fishing stickfloat style on rivers.*

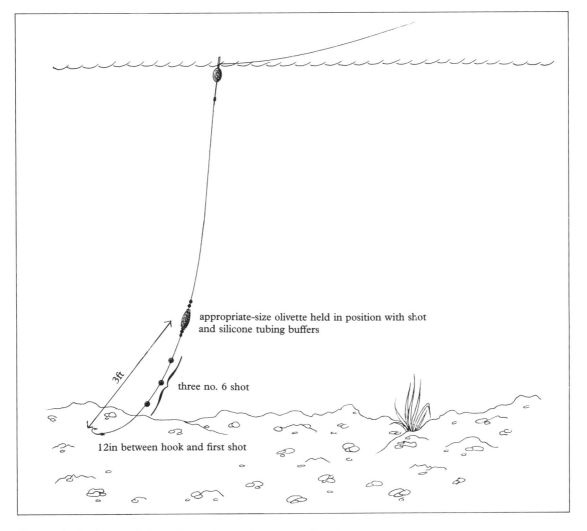

*Shotting for 2g (or larger) floats, for use in very fast or very deep rivers.*

rig; the extra control provided by a long pole should produce far more fish, and lighter, more delicate floats can be used without losing control.

My most frequently used pole float for this style takes 0.6g and is fished on 21–23ft (6.5–7m) of line, so that it can be run for some distance down the peg. The shotting for calm conditions will start with three no. 10s closest to the hook and will be completed with no. 8s. These shot will be at 5–6in (12–15cm) intervals, with the closest one to the hook some

12–18in (30–45cm) away. In very windy conditions better control can be achieved by moving the shot down the line so that they are at 3–4in (7–10cm) intervals.

Sometimes in blustery conditions, or strong flows, I will use a slightly larger float to re-establish my control over the tackle. But bear in mind that if the flow is too fast, the loosefeed will not land within pole range, rendering it ineffective.

When it comes to feeding I will, as with other methods, try to time it so that the hookbait and loosefeed fall together. This will often provide bites, but if it does not, you should start to experiment with the speed and depth of presentation. The pole should make this easy.

Hooks and lines will usually be the same sizes and strengths as they were for still waters. However, the presence of many more large fish, chub for example, would demand an increase in tackle strength, as would powerful flows.

Very fast flows, or extra-deep water, will also demand a return to appropriate-sized olivette rigs. In the case of fast water this will also mean the use of heavy groundbait, or possibly a bait dropper, to get feed down to the bottom within pole range. If the peg is fast enough to need larger floats (2g or more) then I am likely to use an olivette around 3ft (90cm) from the hook and larger drop shot below it, probably three no. 6s. To fish too light in powerful flows would cause the hook to rise well off bottom when the float was held back hard, which would be undesirable if the fish were being kept on the bottom by heavy groundbait.

The float used for this fishing would definitely consist of a body which was wide towards the top, or round. The water pressure on the body helps to keep the float well down in the water when it is held back hard to slow the bait down.

The length of line used with heavy rigs, in fast flows, can be increased to 26ft (8m) or more. This allows the float to be run further down the peg and the extra weight on the line will ensure that it remains easy to control.

### Going after Big Fish

To finish the chapter let us have a look at catching big, powerful fish on the pole. If you have not caught carp, tench or similar fish on the pole, it can be very intimidating, not to mention expensive, if you get it wrong in matches. Using reliable tackle is essential.

The best way to become confident at landing powerful fish on the pole is to go out and practise doing it. But do not go to waters where one or two big fish in a day are all you can

*Pole-bending action from Willow Park Lakes.*

expect, as this will not give you many opportunities to learn during the course of a session. Instead I would suggest using one of the heavily stocked day-ticket waters, which have sprung up around the country.

These are usually stocked with hard-fighting, small- or medium-sized carp. The venue which I use, if I want to practise this kind of fishing, actually holds a huge head of tench and crucians as well; it is Willow Park, near Aldershot. The smaller of the two lakes at this fishery is full of tench, which average at about 2lb each, and crucians, which usually weigh around 1lb.

In the summer, heavy feeding with maggots will bring the fish close to the top to feed and at times they will boil on the surface. Once they are feeding properly it is possible to hook one nearly every time. The float which I use for this very shallow fishing has a wire stem plus bristle, and takes four no. 10 shot. I actually shot it with four pairs of no. 13s which

*Another Willow Park carp is finally beaten.*

seem to give a slightly slower fall. This rig is just a lighter, shallower version of the one which I described for fishing well off bottom at Worsborough Reservoir.

Because you can catch so many powerful fish in a session, working out a reliable set of tackle should not take long. It was practising like this that started me using longer lengths of elastic, to avoid fish 'bottoming out' on it too easily. The main line which I use for this is now usually a 3lb co-polymer line, since a standard line in this strength would be too thick to fish with small, delicate floats. So I use the thinner lines and take great care when attaching shot.

For catching fish up to 3lb or 4lb, I usually settle for a 0.105mm (2lb) hooklength. If the elastic is long enough I suffer very few losses on this. It is usually fished with a Kamasan B520 hook but, if you decide to take my advice and fish one of the heavily stocked carp lakes, check the rules first: barbed hooks are often banned.

If the fish run much bigger than this then you are going to have to step up your tackle even more, bearing in mind that there is a limit to the size of fish you can expect to land on a pole. I know that double-figure fish are sometimes caught but I would suggest that once the fish get past 6lb or 7lb you are going to need luck as well as skill to get them out, and a running-line rig might be more suitable.

Once you have gained confidence in your tackle's ability to land powerful fish, that is, the elastics, lines and hooks, it becomes a simple matter to use this tackle for powerful fish on other venues, just changing to the appropriate floats and shotting – it is that simple.

I shall finish with two final pieces of advice. Firstly, carry several identical rigs if you intend to fish a match for carp, tench, or similar fish. If the hook pulls out of the fish when it has pulled yards of strong elastic from the pole, you are in danger of your terminal tackle tying itself in a huge knot around the end of the pole, as it flies back. Spare rigs can save a lot of wasted retackling time. Secondly, have any spare pole sections placed exactly where you can pick them up without even looking; if you hook a really powerful fish you are likely to need them!

*A fine tench which fell to pole-fished casters.*

# 6　LONG POLE FISHING WITH BLOODWORMS

For anglers who have had little or nothing to do with bloodworm fishing, I realize that it can appear to be highly complicated and full of mystery. In reality the most difficult aspect of bloodworm fishing is getting your hands on a decent supply of the bait: the actual methods should hold no fears.

Because both bloodworms and jokers (their smaller cousins) are most often fed in groundbait or leam (a heavy, sticky, clay-based soil), the rigs used to fish them will usually be designed to get the bait down quickly; use a bulk shot or olivette at a distance of 20–24in (50–60cm) from the hook with one or two no. 10 shot below, positioned 7–8in (17–20cm) from the hook. Sometimes on hard-fished waters I find that I can get better results by swapping the two no. 10s for four no. 13s, set slightly apart. The hook, lines and elastics used should, as always, be carefully balanced to the size of fish being sought.

Floats used often need to be particularly sensitive because the hookbait is often suspended just off bottom, and the fish will feel any resistance from the float as soon as they take the bait. The bait is often fished just off bottom because bloodworms and jokers live in water naturally and can swim. Many of them 'jump' up and down just off bottom, so that is often the best place for your hookbait to be wriggling about, particularly if small fish are your target.

## FEEDING BLOODWORMS

Bloodworms tend to be at their most deadly on waters where they have seen little use: if the fish have not been caught on them, they have no reason to fear them. (The same can also apply to other baits which have not seen much use on a particular water). In these situations the introduction of large quantities of bloodworms and/or jokers at the start of a session will attract a lot of fish, though at times it is difficult to understand why they are not scared by the disturbance caused by the introduction of numerous balls of heavy groundbait!

On venues with a large head of fish, I will feed up to twenty orange-sized balls of groundbait at the start of a session and these might contain 3 pints or more of bloodworms and jokers. This really heavy groundbaiting tends to be aimed at bream. If roach are predominant, smaller quantities, say six or ten balls, are often more productive and 2 pints of jokers will usually be enough for the whole match.

The groundbait should be mixed up well before the match starts. I do not go in for mixing it up the night before, but I do mix it at least half an hour before the start. The reason for this is that the water gradually absorbs into it, so groundbait which feels right when you first mix it will feel too dry ten minutes later and will require more water. You may need to add water two or three times before you are happy with it.

The groundbait, when it is mixed, needs to be stiff enough to carry large quantities of bait without breaking up on impact with the water. A word of warning here: many groundbaits contain salt, which will gradually kill bloodworms, so do not add the bloodworms or jokers to the groundbait until five or ten minutes before the start. If you do add them too early they will 'melt' away. The same applies if you intend to top up the swim with groundbait –

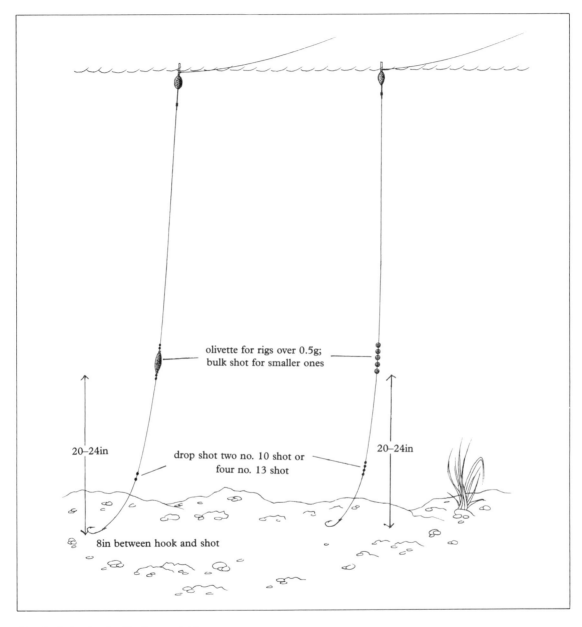

olivette for rigs over 0.5g;
bulk shot for smaller ones

20–24in

20–24in

drop shot two no. 10 shot or
four no. 13 shot

8in between hook and shot

*Standard shotting for bloodworm fishing.*

add your feed to the groundbait a bit at a time, rather than putting it all in together. Incidentally, to spread the jokers evenly through the groundbait mix, it helps if you separate them before adding to the groundbait. To do this add finely sieved damp leam to the jokers (or bloodworms) and mix it in with them: they will then separate, rather than sticking together.

When you have put a large quantity of feed into the peg at the start of the match you will probably not have to top it up for some time. But eventually your catch rate will slow up and you will have to consider feeding again. There are several ways of doing this, but trial and error should quickly teach you which are going to be most productive on your venues.

On some waters you will be able to introduce several large balls of groundbait again, to bring the fish back. However, if the fish are becoming suspicious, it is often better to introduce small balls of groundbait at regular intervals, to cause less disturbance. If this also scares the fish then it might be wise to introduce bloodworms or jokers without groundbait. The easiest way to do this is to add dry grey leam to the jokers, and when they have separated, add a touch of water. The grey leam will become so sticky that the jokers can be rolled into small balls and thrown out without groundbait. Most of them will break up on impact with the water, so do not use this method in running water. If the balls needs to go straight to the bottom, they will have to be tipped in from a cup on the end of the pole to avoid the break-up on impact.

Jokers are used as feed far more than bloodworms, but bloodworms can often be the better feed if you are trying to catch quality fish; bream often fall for bloodworms as feed and so can decent roach. It makes sense when you think about it: if you were trying to catch big roach on a bloodworm-banned venue, big maggots would be more likely bait than squatts. The principle is the same: bigger fish often go for slightly bigger bait.

## GLOUCESTER AND HOLME PIERREPONT

An excellent example of this came during the early days of bloodworm fishing on the Gloucester Canal. I was using bloodworms as both feed and hookbait, with the result that I consistently caught roach in the 2–10oz range. Obviously I also caught some tiny fish, but the bulk of my weight came from decent fish; the biggest I landed on bloodworm weighed 1lb 11oz! Most of the other anglers were using jokers as feed and they were catching much smaller fish.

*A roach is swung in by an angler competing in a match at Holme Pierrepont.*

Often their biggest fish were only 3oz, so they had to catch far more fish to compete with me. To catch the better fish I was also fishing on the bottom, with double bloodworms on the hook. It is not unusual for the better fish to fall to bloodworms fished slightly over depth, particularly when they are fed instead of the more active jokers.

The method that I developed at Gloucester was also to win me a big invitation event at Holme Pierrepont, Nottinghamshire.

The match in question was the 1988 Van Den Eynde Classic, formerly the Central TV Classic. Usually this event is dominated by big bream weights, but during that summer far fewer bream were showing and the top weight was not likely to be above 20lb. One of my team mates, Wayne Swinscoe, told me that he thought my way of fishing for roach could be very dangerous, so I decided to try it.

This venue is much shallower than the canal, so my 1g Gloucester float was swapped for a 0.4g model, which was much more suitable for 5ft (1.5m) of water. The feeding remained the same, and I stuck to double bloodworms as bait, though the fish were comparatively small and I caught most of them with the bait just off bottom, rather than on it. When I topped up my feed the fish would accept several balls at a time, so I only had to top up three times during the whole match! This was very useful as it left both hands free to catch the fish. I ended with 16lb 11oz, winning with just a few ounces to spare; this was one of my most memorable victories.

## WHEN THE FISHING GETS HARD

On hard-fished bloodworm venues, particularly smaller ones like canals, the fish can stop

*England International Alan Scotthorne in action at Holme Pierrepont, Nottingham.*

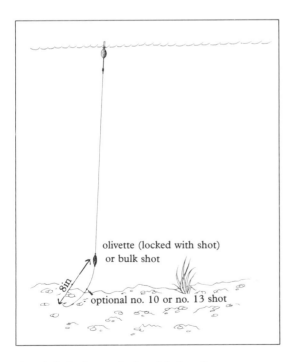

*Speed rig for bottom-feeding fish (usually gudgeon and ruffe) used with bloodworms.*

olivette (locked with shot) or bulk shot

8in

optional no. 10 or no. 13 shot

responding to the heavy bombardment of groundbait at the start of a session, so the feeding needs to become more subtle to achieve the best results. There are several possible ways to introduce these smaller quantities of feed.

The most obvious possibility is simply to start by throwing in fewer balls of groundbait. If this is still too much I would switch to feeding with a plastic cup on the end of the pole. If the fish still accept some groundbait, far less will be needed to hold the bloodworms or jokers together if it is carefully tipped into the water from a cup. This method of feeding also causes far less disturbance and allows the feed to be placed very accurately. If a dozen balls are thrown in, one or two landing in the wrong place is not the end of the world: however, if only two or three balls are introduced, it can be essential that they land in exactly the right place.

In situations where the fish only accept small quantities of bait, the tackle which you use to catch them is likely to be at its most refined,

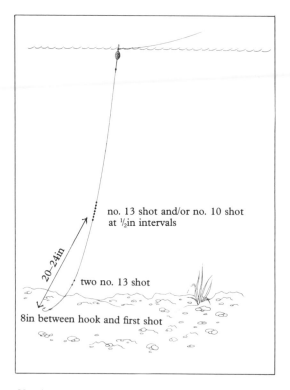

no. 13 shot and/or no. 10 shot at ½in intervals

two no. 13 shot

20–24in

8in between hook and first shot

*Shotting variation for shy bloodworm-eating fish.*

as the fish are almost certain to be extremely wary. Wire-bristled floats, dotted right down, are likely to see most action, and the hooks and hooklengths will probably be some of the finest you are ever going to use. Hooklengths should be 0.05mm diameter, and my hook patterns for this fishing are most often Gamakatsu 6311s or 6313s.

In shallow canals, where this situation is most likely to be encountered, my shotting would usually consist of two no. 13 shot, at 1in (2.5cm) intervals, and 8in (20cm) from the hook, and the rest of the shot at the usual 20–24in (50–60cm) from the hook. But these shot would be kept tiny, no. 10s and 13s, and they would be attached to the line at ½in (12mm) intervals, which seems to work well when very shy fish are being sought.

It often pays to feed a number of different spots when the fishing gets this hard. I often carefully tip two or three small balls of feed into three or four different spots. Each spot will have been carefully plumbed, and the depth marked on the pole, so that I can move from area to area without getting the depths wrong. It is often possible to catch several fish from each spot in turn, thus building a weight while other anglers, fishing only area, struggle to keep the fish. When bites dry up in a particular spot, another tiny ball of feed can be tipped in from the pole cup and you can then fish another area while the fish resettle on the new feed. But be warned: in situations like this fish can be easily overfed, so top up sparingly – particularly in winter. Half a pint of jokers can often cover you for the whole match.

If the fish refuse to accept groundbait, a pole cup can be used to feed neat bloodworms or jokers into the swim. This can be deadly but it does have its limitations, especially in flowing water, where it is a non-starter. Deep water can also be a problem as jokers, in particular, will spread over a very large area by the time they reach the bottom. With this in mind, the best way to feed neat bloodworms and jokers in deep water is with a bait dropper.

Alternatively, you can use leam to stick jokers together. Some types of leam are stickier than others and you will need to experiment to establish exactly how much to use. Most fish will accept leam and you should also note that by sticking to the jokers, even after they have broken apart on the bottom, it stops them from swimming out of the peg as quickly as neat jokers can. If the fish will put up with a lot of disturbance you can try feeding the jokers or bloodworms in large balls made from soil that includes clay or leam. If mixed correctly the balls can be made to break up slowly, gradually releasing the bait to the fish.

## CATCHING FISH NEAR THE SURFACE

As with other baits there are days when fishing bloodworms on or near the bottom will not work because the fish insist on feeding closer to the surface. This is most likely to happen on deep venues during very hot weather. The 1992 *Angling Times* winter league final, which was fished on the lake at Roundhay Park, Leeds, is an excellent example of this.

This venue varies wildly in depth. The shallower areas were no problem, as the fish were feeding near the bottom. But the deep areas were totally different, for the fish did not want to be near the bottom of 12ft (3.5m) of water: instead they were much happier to feed 3–4ft (90–120cm) from the surface. To keep them there the feed needed to be regular, so I ended up feeding jokers held together in very soft groundbait which formed a cloud as soon as it hit the water. The rigs used were the same as the type which I have already described for fishing well off bottom with other baits, that is, using very light shotting. The closest shot to the hook would usually be no further than 12in (30cm). Bloodworm is such a delicate bait that to move the shot much further away would almost certainly result in the bait being sucked without a bite registering.

On the day of the final I actually drew a peg with 8ft (2.4m) of water. I could catch neither on, or just off bottom, nor could I catch 3ft or 4ft (90–120cm) deep. Instead I eventually won my section by fishing 12in (30cm) off bottom. If I had not experimented with the depth, I would have failed. If you are not catching, always look for sensible changes to try.

Apart from depth, there are other variations which you can try in order to attract bites. On slow-moving water you can try the usual variations of speed of presentation: hold the float back by varying degrees, so that the bait goes through the swim at different speeds. Twitching the bait also works extremely well at times: moving the float upwards, or sideways, by an inch or two will cause the bait to jump in much the same way that the jokers you have fed will be doing. This action can provoke fish to grab the bait quickly, possibly because they think it is going to swim away from them. Sometimes an occasional twitch will work best, while on other days almost continual move-

ment will succeed. I have actually watched the response of fish in cold, clear water: when the bait was suspended in front of them it was ignored, but if it was moved up and down they took it.

To make the bait behave naturally great care should be taken to make sure that your hookbait is as lively as possible. Bloodworms are much more delicate than maggots, so need protecting from the sun and wind. I tend to keep my hookbait well wrapped up and in the shade, or in a cool box in really hot weather; I only get it out a bit at a time, so that not all of my supply is exposed to the elements for the full duration of the session.

Fishing bloodworms in ones or twos is also not necessarily the best approach. When large quantities of feed have been introduced the biggest fish will often go around 'hoovering up' large quantities. To catch these fish a bunch a bloodworms will be a more appealing, and still natural, bait. Do not ignore this possibility if you are after quality fish.

## ALTERNATIVE BAITS

Another hookbait variation that can be unbeatable at times is to use jokers instead of bloodworms. This tends to work best on heavily fished venues where the fish have been caught many times on bloodworms. If jokers are the normal feed the fish eventually work out that jokers are safe to eat, but that the larger bloodworms are not. The change to jokers on the hook can fool them, at least for a while.

Knowing that you need to use jokers is one thing, efficiently baiting the hook with them is another. I have no problem with putting jokers on the hook, but having witnessed many other anglers struggling to do it, I would strongly suggest practising this before attempting to tackle a match with jokers for hookbait. The best way to become efficient at baiting the hook is simply to sit down and practise it continually. That is, do not actually fish; just bait the hook, and then remove the bait. Repeat this over and over again until it becomes easy. Of course, an efficient tackle layout is also essential (*see* Chapter 5).

Finally, watch out for fish reverting back to other baits. If everyone on a venue is catching on bloodworms the fish will eventually forget to be wary of maggots. Keep your eyes open for these changes, since the first fish to show a preference for other baits are usually the quality ones – and they are often the match winners. On many venues it is possible to start off fishing bloodworms or jokers, and change later to maggots or casters, which will have been fed from the start. This way large quantities of smaller fish can be caught early on and larger ones can be caught later. Often switching between the two baits is best.

There are also venues which just do not seem to respond properly to bloodworms and jokers. The river Cam is a prime example: bloodworms can produce a few tiny fish when the going is exceptionally tough, but no one ever puts a big weight together on it (at least not up to now). Some very good anglers try it, but it is so unproductive that the vast majority do not even consider taking bloodworms along. Bearing in mind that roach are the venue's main species, it is a strange situation. Why do the fish still get caught on maggots, pinkies and bread, yet refuse to try a succulent new bait which they have not been caught on? It does not make much sense.

The same situation can occur elsewhere. For example, in 1993 I fished an invitation event on Cleethorpes boating lake, which is a shallow,

nicely coloured venue, with a large head of small roach. Bloodworms were so unsuccessful in practice sessions that very few teams even bothered to take any on the day of the match: yet the venue seemed ideal for them, and I would be very surprised if the lake did not hold some bloodworms naturally.

Cases like these are the exception, rather than the rule. I still stand by what I said earlier: bloodworms tend to be at their most deadly on waters where they have seen little use. I remember fishing matches at Edgbaston Reservoir, Birmingham, where bloodworms are usually banned. Without bloodworms it was often difficult to catch an odd pound or two of roach and perch, with some areas appearing all but devoid of fish. On the odd occasions when bloodworms were allowed the transition was startling. The introduction of several balls of feed would send the fish into a feeding frenzy, and most anglers experienced bites all day on their way to large weights of small roach and perch.

Most open-match venues, where they are allowed, have already been tried out with bloodworms. But if you fish a club water with a suitable fish population, where no one has bothered, give bloodworm fishing a go – it will almost certainly work.

To conclude, remember that bloodworms and jokers are not incredibly difficult to fish. The rigs are not vastly different from those used for other baits and, if you follow my guidelines, you should be able to master the bait with limited problems.

# 7  POLE FISHING TO HAND (WHIP FISHING)

When the match angler is faced with catching large quantities of small (and sometimes decent) fish, the quickest way to catch them is often by fishing 'to hand'; this involves using a pole that has a line attached which is almost as long as the pole, so that the fish can be swung in without taking off any sections. The poles designed specifically for this type of fishing (for small fish) are known as 'whips' because of the very fine soft flexible tips, which are usually used instead of elastic.

The line is attached directly to the tip of the pole. There are several ways to do this; for example, stonfo connectors, which are glued on to the end of the pole are effective. Alternatively, a loop can be tied in the end of the line, through which the line below is then pushed, creating another loop. This second loop is put over the pole tip and pulled tight. Two pieces of plastic tubing must be threaded on to the line before the loops are formed: the first of these is pushed down the pole tip to hold the loop attachment in place; the line between the two pieces of tubing is then wound several times around the pole tip and, finally, the second piece of tubing is slid over the very tip of the pole. As long as the tubing fits tightly, there is no danger of the knot slipping off. Some whip tips are fitted with a piece of cord which extends from the tip and has a knot in it. If the same sliding loop is passed behind the knot and then pulled tight, the line will be safely secured.

All three attachment methods are fine. I tend to use the stonfo or the knotted cord but would be just as happy using the two pieces of tubing.

The whips that I carry are up to 7m long. Some anglers use them up to 11m, a size com-

*A small roach is swung to land on the Gloucester Canal.*

monly used in other countries, particularly Italy. But Italian weather is a lot less windy than we are used to and, unless the float used is very heavy, 11m of line will often be all but unfishable. By all means try the extra-long whips and decide their practicality for yourself, but as I do not use them, I cannot really write about them!

## BLEAK FISHING

My bleak rigs do not come out half as often as they used to. In the past many of our rivers

*A tench, caught on casters, is safely landed.*

were teeming with these tiny silver fish to the point where getting a bait through them to bigger fish underneath, was all but impossible. Now there are comparatively few venues which hold a large enough head of bleak to make big weights possible, but they still play their part in results, particularly on coloured rivers.

Getting bites from bleak, when they are present in quantity, is usually easy. Converting bites into fish in the net is not quite so straightforward. There can be few match anglers who have not experienced a shoal of bleak boiling on the surface as soon as bait is thrown in. With a conventional float the vast majority of bites are missed, as the fish grab the hookbait and reject it with lightning speed. To overcome this problem I use a rig which is totally different to anything else which I have covered in the

book so far; the float becomes nothing more than a casting weight and the line is watched for bites.

## The Greased-Line Method

I was first told of this style many, many years ago, when I was still a junior. Unfortunately I did not quite manage to grasp the subtleties of the method straight away. I knew that the float needed to be of a heavy material, so I used a 6in (15cm) piece of cane; but I had not understood that the line needed to be greased, so that it could be seen on the surface. The end product was, in effect, a bolt rig for bleak. The bites would be signalled by the float's desperate efforts to cock, or slide along the surface. Fortunately, I improved on my initial attempts at bleak fishing, and the greased-line method which I am now going to outline is of far more use to me.

The 'float' takes the form of a piece of cane which, in the case of my rigs, is approximately 5cm long and 3mm thick. It is fastened to the line by a piece of silicone tubing at each end. The cane's purpose is to provide casting weight; other materials will also do the job – I used to use lengths of porcupine quill.

The line above the cane will be the same as it is on other rigs – either 1lb or 1½lb. But below the float we encounter something different: a 3ft (90cm) length of invisible mending thread. This is very similar to ordinary line, but if it is run between finger and thumbnail it crinkles up, forming lots of coils. When the line is greased, these lie on the surface, and bites are indicated by the coils straightening and being pulled under. This form of bite indication prevents the fish from feeling the float and consequently rejecting the bait. The hooklength is attached at the end of the invisible thread. The strength of the hooklength (and size of hook) depends on just how ravenously the fish are feeding. I normally start with a 1lb hooklength and a size 20 hook; this could be varied in either direction.

The crinkled section of invisible thread is, as

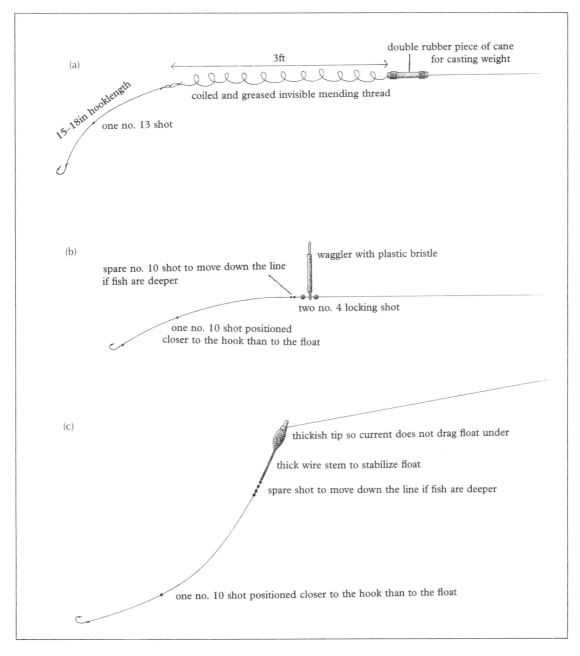

(a)

double rubber piece of cane
for casting weight

3ft

coiled and greased invisible mending thread

15–18in hooklength

one no. 13 shot

(b)

waggler with plastic bristle

spare no. 10 shot to move down the line
if fish are deeper

two no. 4 locking shot

one no. 10 shot positioned
closer to the hook than to the float

(c)

thickish tip so current does not drag float under

thick wire stem to stabilize float

spare shot to move down the line if fish are deeper

one no. 10 shot positioned closer to the hook than to the float

*Bleak rigs. (a) Greased-line rig; (b) Mini-waggler rig; (c) Top-and-bottom rig for 'boiling' water.*

I have already mentioned, treated with some form of flotant. If this flotant gets on to the actual hooklength problems can be encountered, with the bait refusing to sink naturally.

My hooklengths will usually be in the region of 15–18in (38–45cm) for this style of fishing. I do not want the bait stopping only a couple of inches under the surface, so I attach a no.

13 shot to the hooklength – this easily over-comes any problems caused by floatant.

On some days it is possible to see the hook-bait under the surface when you are fishing this style. If this is the case I would advise you to watch the maggot instead of the line – if the maggot disappears, you strike. Under these cir-cumstances the fish have even less time to reject the bait.

Occasionally, even when watching the line, bleak bites can be too fast to hit. If this happens you can always resort to a counting technique, very similar to the one which I discussed for dace on the waggler (*see* Chapter 2). Simply keep casting the tackle and striking, varying the time between the two, until you settle on a time lag which increases your catch rate.

When I strike and fail to connect with a fish, I swing the tackle around behind me and bang it back out. Underhand swings tend to be much slower.

Feeding is also critical and will need to be carried out left-handed (presuming you are holding the pole with your right). I always wear a bait apron when speed fishing for bleak and, every time I cast with my right hand, I use the left hand to take a pinch of maggots from the apron and throw them to the catching area. Because of the speed of the bites, it is not unusual to be swinging in a fish whilst you are still feeding. Co-ordination is therefore vital.

Incidentally, if the fish are feeding particu-larly well, you can also catch a number of fish on one maggot; sometimes they will continue to take the bait when it is little more than a piece of skin. This, of course, saves an awful lot of rebaiting time over five hours, which can be used to catch more fish.

Bleak are not the only species which can fall to this method. On a number of occasions I have caught large quantities of dace on the greased-line rig; and I can remember a practice session on the Thames at Lechlade, during which the bleak were pushed out of the peg by roach and perch, many of which were over 8oz. I was catching them that day on just 3m of pole, and I certainly did not expect the roach

and perch to feed just under the surface at such short range.

On another occasion, again on the Thames, I was fishing for bleak in a match on a very hot summer's day, when few decent fish were being caught. Late in the event, large, dark shapes became visible underneath the feed: a shoal of chub had moved in. I realized that I had little chance of landing one on a whip, so I took the rig off and reattached it to a running-line float rod. I went on to win with a bleak haul which included two bonus chub of over $2\frac{1}{2}$lb each. Bleak definitely are not the only species which can fall to this method!

In general, the more bleak there are present, the closer you will be able to catch them. Usually, if they are one of my targets, I will set up whips of two or three different lengths; then I start on the shortest, and if the bleak move out I can follow them.

### When the Greased-Line Rig Fails

Strong winds can make the greased-line method ineffective. If this is the case I will usually change to a tiny, bottom-end-only, wag-gler-type float; one taking two no. 4 shot is usually about right. If I am fishing shallow, about 18in (45cm) deep, I will use just one no. 10 shot down the line, but more no. 10s will be included in the shot which lock the float in position. If I start to fish deeper these can then be brought into play. When bleak are feeding deeper the bites are usually much easier to hit; if you are casting directly on top of the feed area and missing instant bites, it is worth con-sidering casting upstream of the feed, so that the bait is deeper in the water by the time it reaches the fish.

The waggler for this type of fishing needs to be very sensitive to try to avoid fish dropping the bait, and the ones I use are fitted with a plastic bristle.

If the bleak insist on feeding several feet below the surface on days when the wind is only light, I would revert to a standard, bristle-type, top-and-bottom pole float, probably of around 0.25g. This would be fished with a string of shot on the line, just like the 'on the drop' rigs described in chapter 6. These last two rigs I have mentioned are also used for small fish of other species; it is not unusual for small roach, perch, rudd and others to feed well off bottom within whip range, particularly when near-bank weed-beds offer them some cover.

I also fish top-and-bottom for bleak in highly coloured rain-affected rivers which are boiling due to the speed of the water. In these conditions the fish often feed close to the surface, but do not actually grab the bait the second it hits the water. This means that bites can usually be hit on a conventional float, so the top-and-bottom float can be used to control the bait through the peg. However, because of the boiling water conditions, I do not use a bristle float. Instead I use a float with a thin, buoyant balsa tip (so that the currents do not keep dragging it under) and a comparatively heavy wire stem, to help stabilize it. Shotting it similar to the mini-waggler rig: with one no. 10 below the float in shallow depths, but more shot directly underneath the float in case they are needed.

Feeding will still be carried out every cast, and I will try to get away with using big maggots rather than pinkies. If you can catch on maggots the fish are usually of better quality, around thirty to the pound instead of forty-five. I know which size I would prefer to catch!

## GUDGEON AND RUFFE

On many canals gudgeon and ruffe provide a target for the whip. Usually this means fishing on or near the bottom, often with bloodworms, if allowed.

The rigs I generally use for these bottom-feeding species have an olivette (or bulk shot) just 8in (20cm) from the hook. Sometimes there will be no drop shot below this; but if there is, it will be a no. 10 or no. 13, placed on the actual hooklength – one of the very few situations where I ever place a shot on a hooklength.

These rigs will get the bait down close to the bottom very quickly, and then let it fall slowly for the last few inches. The size of the float varies from 0.25g to 1g: the lighter ones will be used for comparatively shy-biting fish, in situations where the float is easy to control, for example under the pole tip or in very calm conditions. The larger sizes are used for getting the bait down very fast to freely feeding fish, or keeping control over the bait in windy conditions. If wind is causing you problems by blowing the line, you can always sink the line by swinging the tackle out to maximum range, then pulling it sharply back towards you with the pole tip under the water.

In very windy conditions it can be worth considering a switch to a bottom-end-only, waggler-type float. I would use one of the all-balsa, fine-tipped floats which I mentioned in Chapter 2. Shotting would be with an olivette or bulk shot, close to the hook. The float might need to change, but the shotting does not.

The hooks used for these rigs are most likely to be fine wire 24s and 22s, tied to a 0.07mm diameter line.

If I am bloodworm fishing the depth is likely to be set so that the bait is fractionally off bottom. Do not ignore the possibility of trying just over depth, particularly if you are missing bites, or failing to attract any bites at all during conditions when the water is very cold.

When feeding jokers, for gudgeon, it is important to establish whether the fish like groundbait or not. Usually they do, but on some heavily fished venues they do not. If ruffe are the predominant species groundbait is far more likely to be a non-starter as, in my experience, they are not very keen on it. If groundbait is not going to be used, soil, leam, or a mixture of the two, can be used instead to get the jokers to the bottom. If I use soil, it is collected from molehills and then riddled. Once you have got it to a nice, fine consistency it can be used in exactly the same way as groundbait.

On a venue where gudgeon or ruffe are prolific, I would usually start with two or three egg-sized balls of groundbait/soil (loaded with jokers) and then top up as necessary. This will often be on a regular basis, with small pieces, if they will accept it. On harder venues extra feed may have to be introduced with caution.

If you are fishing on these harder, lower-weight venues, make sure that the whip is definitely the best method. Fishing past the pole tip never gives the same control as using a longer pole, with a short line: so, even for gudgeon and ruffe, a short-line rig fished at 5–6m, can be better than fishing 3m or 4m to hand, in low-weight matches.

When bloodworms are banned, squatt or pinkie fishing for gudgeon is possible, using small, regular pieces of groundbait with a just a few squatts in them. The hookbait should be fished just over depth and perhaps the olivette, or shot, will have to be moved slightly further from the hook for the fish to accept the bait properly. Ruffe are not usually caught so effectively on squatts. If bloodworms are banned, redworms are more likely to be the best bait, fished with a short line (*see* Chapter 10).

When you are deciding how far out to fish for gudgeon and ruffe, bear in mind some general rules. To start with, warmer water will see the fish move towards the shallows; colder water will encourage them to retreat to the depths. Water colour also affects them; heavily coloured water will again have them heading for the shallows, with clearer water encouraging them to look for the security of deeper water. So at one extreme of these conditions – a canal in the middle of a hot summer, with boat traffic keeping the water heavily coloured – fish will be found very close to the banks, and often a pole of 2m or less will suffice. At the other end of the scale, in the same canal in the depths of a cold winter without boats to colour the water, the deepest part of the peg is likely to be the most prolific area.

The decision on where to fish is not always this straightforward. A freezing cold canal which is still heavily coloured, will have you scratching your head, trying to work out a sensible compromise.

If big fish are likely to be caught in amongst

*The elastic does its job on another powerful fish.*

the gudgeon or ruffe, I will switch to a pole with elastic, fished to hand, instead of a whip. A good example of this would be on the Gloucester Canal when I am fishing 3m to hand on top of the near shelf. This area is usually around 6ft (1.8m) deep and certainly capable of producing fish of over 1lb. Fish of this size are a huge bonus and could prove to be very difficult to land on a whip, so I do not take any chances.

A second example of this is the largest lake at Willow Park, near Aldershot. Here large quantities of small perch can sometimes be caught by fishing only 3–4m to hand. Most of the perch could be safely landed on a whip – but I am not so sure about the tench and carp, which are likely to join in. Elastic certainly gets my vote, and the speed element of fishing to hand is also important.

## BREAD PUNCH FISHING

Another bait that sees a lot of use in conjuction

*A good fish comes to the net.*

with whips is bread, usually in punched form.

The main target species on bread punch are usually roach and small skimmers: fish which are easily handled without elastic. The venues where bread punch works are typically either canals or slow-moving rivers, such as the Cam or the old course of the River Nene. These are small rivers where the fish are often within range of whips. On larger rivers bread punch can often work best further out from the bank on a running-line rig.

On a river, 5m is the length of whip that I most often use. This is usually long enough to reach a decent depth, and benefit from some flow. I would rarely fish shorter than this on a river, but I would go longer if I thought it would help.

The tackle used is going to be fairly positive; if I am fishing to hand I am looking for a decent weight. So the hook is usually a size 20, big enough for few fish to come off, and it is silver in colour to help merge in with the bait. The

hooklength will be 0.09mm (co-polymer of course), which gives a hook and line combination suitable for continually lifting out 2oz or 3oz fish, if necessary.

Unless the water is exceptionally deep I will settle for a pole float taking 0.75g. This will be fished to get the bait down to the fish quickly, with an olivette about 20in (50cm) from the hook and two no. 10 shot 8in (20cm) from it. The hook will be set slightly off bottom at the start of the session, but can later be set either shallower or deeper to attract more bites. Bites can come very quickly using this method, with the bait being taken down so fast, so thoughtful organization is required to enable you to refill the punch and feed in a very short time.

Under my own system, I hold the pole in my right hand, with the hook between thumb and forefinger. The left hand holds the ready-loaded punch. The sequence is then as follows: bait the hook from the punch; let go of the hook and allow the tackle to swing out (the float is heavy enough to do this underhand); refill the punch from the slice of bread which is on my left-hand side; drop the punch and move the pole from right hand to left; watch the float while squeezing and throwing a small ball of groundbait with my right hand; transfer the pole back to right hand and continue to watch float. If a bite comes while I am still feeding groundbait, I strike left-handed and move the pole back to my right hand while swinging the fish in.

The need to refill the punch is the main difference between speed fishing with bread and speed fishing with other baits. It might not sound like much of a difference, but when bites are coming quickly you will soon discover the need to practise it.

The size of punch used will need to be varied. A big piece of bread is more likely to attract the attentions of quality fish, but lots of extra bites from smaller fish can make a small punch more practical. You will have to experiment during the course of a session to establish the optimum size on the day.

The groundbait used for this style is likely to

be pure bread of some sort. I currently use liquidized bread (which I sieve to remove any lumps), mixed with standard white groundbait. The faster the flow, the higher the percentage of ordinary groundbait. The reason for this is that liquidized bread usually floats for a few seconds, then sinks slowly, breaking up as it does so. Once the groundbait is added to liquidized bread, and then slightly wetted, it will sink and can thus be induced to break up much closer to the bottom.

I usually start a river session by feeding every cast, but then I play the situation by ear. Cutting back to once every two casts is my most common approach; to continue feeding every cast runs the risk of over-feeding. If the fish go away, I can always step up the feed to try to attract them back. If they refuse to return I often start fishing further over with either a long pole or a running-line rod, possibly using bread still, but more likely with another bait. If they were desperate for bread they would have moved to the whip line.

If you do decide to fish a long pole with bread, the float can be smaller, but the positioning of the shot/olivette would remain similar. If you are on the short-line method because bites are scarce, and more control is needed to attract them, it is also worth considering scaling down the hook and hooklength to a size 22 tied to a 0.07mm line.

This same scaling down of tackle also applies to most bread punch fishing on canals, where the target weights and size of fish are smaller to start with. If fishing to hand on canals, 0.4g would probably be most useful. Incidentally, as with other whip rigs, bottom-end-only floats can be used to overcome strong winds.

The feed on canals depends largely on the size of the fish. Liquidized bread will be fine for decent weights, or decent fish, but a very fine groundbait with no liquidized bread can be best if the fish are tiny – you do not want to fill them up. Even if I am feeding liquidized bread on a canal, I am likely to use it sparingly, probably feeding once, then fishing over it until bites dry up; only then would I feed again.

Alternatively, when using a very fine groundbait for tiny fish, I would try to keep a cloud in the water by feeding regular tiny dabs.

One final point: bread punch fishing can work in coloured water but, traditionally, it is far more deadly when the water is comparatively clear.

## FISHING FOR HUGE WEIGHTS

To finish the chapter I am going to look at a style which just about falls into the category of whip fishing: this is the fishing-to-hand style required to catch huge weights from the prolific venues found in places like Scandinavia or Ireland, where 100lb hauls are common.

Not surprisingly the tackle for this style of fishing has to be stepped up dramatically, starting with the pole. The fine-tipped whips are not going to be of any use for this fishing; instead the line needs to be attached to the tip of a normal pole, but without elastic.

For my own poles I have separate top sections, which have been cut back slightly and then fitted with a loop of very thick line, which is whipped to the pole tip and then glued in position. The loop then extends from the end of the pole, and the main line is attached directly to this. In the past I have also got away with removing the elastic from a pole top-section and replacing it with strong line, so that it runs through the pole and, again, has the main line attached directly to it. This method is worth considering if you do not have enough separate pole tops to enable you to change some permanently. I would still advise you to reinforce the very tip of the pole if you decide to run the line through it: about an inch of whipping should do the job.

The pole itself also needs to be strong enough to lift out a 1lb-plus fish without breaking. Do not think that every pole can handle this style – many cannot and breakages are expensive. You have been warned!

The length of pole that you are going to be fishing with will vary from venue to venue. If the fish come close enough for 6m or 7m, it is easy. Once you get up to lengths of 9m or more, many anglers encounter problems, particularly if they have to stand up to fish, which is the case on some venues where extensive reed-beds demand that you wade out past the normal knee-height depth.

If you have never done this type of fishing with the longer lengths of pole, I would recommend that you practise handling the tackle on one of your local waters before even travelling abroad. Just swinging out the tackle and lifting it back in, with 9m or 10m poles, will give you an idea of the hard work involved over a five-hour match. You will also start to appreciate the size of float required in windy conditions.

For fishing 6m or 7m to hand a 4g float may well be enough, but for the longer poles 6–10g floats are more likely to be appropriate. The shotting should be kept very simple to avoid tangles: one large bulk shot/olivette and a single drop shot below. To keep everything in balance this single shot should be at least a no. 4, possibly a BB.

Hooks are at least size 14, preferably with a longish shank to help unhooking, tied to line of at least $2\frac{1}{2}$lb breaking strain. Main lines should be at least 4lb breaking strain. All of the lines will be standard rather than co-polymer.

Floats will be armed with thick bristles, and I use a piece of silicone tubing on the base of the bristle (with the line passing through it). This takes a lot of the strain away from the ring on the side of the float, which can otherwise decide to pull out at inconvenient moments, such as in mid-match.

If you sit in a position which is well off the water, casting involves just letting go of the hook and swinging the tackle out underhand. If you are fishing from water level this is not so easy with long poles, as the terminal tackle hits the water on the way out. In these circumstances I use a sideways swing, which I find very effective; many others prefer to cast overhead.

Feeding has to be done efficiently as the float is settling. Stiff groundbait is usually used, in

*The author's catch of 11lb 4oz was good enough for second place in the 1988 pole fishing championship on the Gloucester Canal.*

order to keep the fish down on the bottom. To feed this, I switch the pole from right to left hand, then squeeze and throw the groundbait right-handed. The groundbait will usually be full of casters and, if bream are present, worms. Huge quantities of bait can be used on these prolific venues. A gallon of casters alone is certainly not out of place and I would want to have at least 20lb of groundbait with me.

The hookbaits are usually either a bunch of red maggots for roach or worms for bream. For roach the bait would usually be set at the exact depth while for bream I would expect to fish slightly over depth.

With all these forms of speed fishing a smooth, well thought-out, controlled approach is required. Frantic attempts at extra speed are usually counter-productive and often result in tangles, breakages, lost fish and lost time. It is far better to concentrate on efficiency; as you settle into a steady rhythm the speed will usually take care of itself!

# FEEDER FISHING

Swimfeeders offer an extremely effective way of placing the hookbait right next to an angler's feed, particularly at long range or in strong flows, but also at much more moderate ranges where the hookbait and feed need to be kept in one small area.

On some venues the fish eventually become scared of feeders, especially if they have been caught on them many times. However, they remain a deadly method for many species, on a wide range of waters. The various situations where they are most useful are discussed below.

## CHUB

The chub's liking for the far banks of rivers makes it an obvious candidate for the feeder. Many far banks are well out of range of loose-feed, so the feeder comes into its own. But there are also plenty of days when the feeder will outscore float methods even when the river is flowing at a comfortable float-fishing pace and the fish are within loosefeed range.

### Necessary Equipment

If the river is wide, and the far bank needs to be reached, a long powerful carbon rod is needed. The one I use is 13ft long. My reel would be loaded with a 3lb line and to avoid 'crack-offs' due to the force of the cast, I would also use a shock leader. This is simply a length of stronger line (I usually use 5lb) which extends from the feeder down on to the reel spool before casting. This strong line will then take the extra strain of the powerful, long-range cast, but the 3lb main line will cause far less

*The best fish from a mixed haul taken from the Gloucester Canal.*

friction as it runs through the rings. It will also provide less of a target for cross-winds to get hold of, so longer casts can be made than if the reel was loaded with a 5lb line. (For fishing at more comfortable ranges I would switch to a slightly softer, 11ft or 12ft rod and also dispense with the shock leader. The rod's ability to cushion the plunges of big fish is more important than its casting ability at these moderate ranges.)

For long-range casting the shock leader is joined to the main line with a full blood knot. At the other end of the shock leader I tie on my feeder. There are two main set-ups you can use: a fixed paternoster set-up (which is my

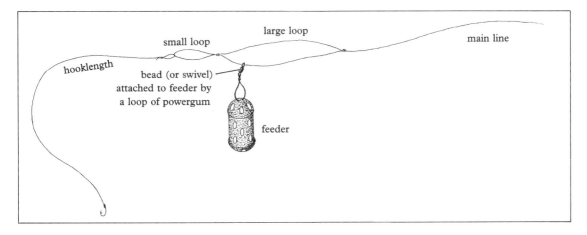

*'Loop' method of feeder fishing.*

preferred method) or the more fashionable 'loop' method.

For the latter method, the feeder needs to have a small swivel or bead attached to it, so that it can slide freely up and down the line. To tackle up, the main reel line is first passed through the swivel; then a large fixed loop is tied in the line in such a way that the feeder is attached inside this loop (I use the same figure-of-eight knot which I use for making loops in hooklengths); another small loop is then tied into the end of this large loop in such a way that the feeder can slide between the two knots; the hooklength is then attached to the small loop, by my normal loop-to-loop method.

The idea is for the fish to be able to move off with the bait without feeling the feeder. If

the feeder has much weight attached it can also act as a self-hooking rig: when the feeder makes contact with the back end of the main loop, the sudden resistance should hook the fish.

This method can be particularly successful when an angler is struggling to hit fast-biting species – such as dace or silver bream.

With the fixed paternoster the feeder cannot slide on the line and the hooklength is tied to the main line above the feeder. The distance between the feeder and the hooklength junction knot varies; but as a general rule, the faster the water the shorter the distance.

My hooklengths are in two parts; the length of line which is actually joined to the main line has a loop tied in the end of it, then the proper hooklength is attached to this by the loop-to-

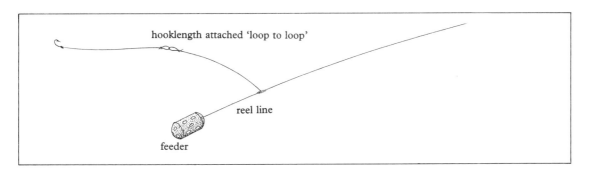

*Fixed paternoster set-up.*

loop method. The first section of the hook-length is the same breaking strain as the main line, while the strength of the line to which the hook is actually tied can be varied as required.

For chub fishing the hooklength is typically a standard 1½lb, or 2lb if the feeder is particularly heavy: fishing with a heavy feeder in conjunction with light hooklengths is a good way to be broken on the bite. I also tend to steer clear of the co-polymer hooklengths when heavy-feeder fishing for the same reason. The hooks themselves need to be pretty strong for chub: Kamasan B520 or Drennan chub hooks are currently my standard choice.

### Dealing with Bites

Bite indication will vary with the speed of the flow. In slow-moving water I would use a soft quivertip to show the bites, and look for decent pull-rounds as the fish pick up the bait and move off with it. For fishing like this I usually keep the rod low to the water and try to position it so that the line comes away from the tip at something close to 90 degrees. Obviously if the fish picks up the bait and swims towards you, the tip will drop back to indicate a bite when the fish moves the feeder.

In faster flows the rod needs to be positioned differently to show bites. Angle it high in the air, pointing downstream and slightly to the front. This keeps most of the line off the water, thus stopping the water pressure on the line moving the feeder.

There are then two main ways to set about connecting with bites. The first involves adding or subtracting weight from the feeder, until it only just holds bottom (this can be achieved with various clip-on weights). The idea of this is that a fish taking the bait will move the feeder very easily, so the quivertip (which needs to be fairly stiff in these circumstances) will immediately straighten as the feeder rolls downriver and allows the line to go slack. Some bites will also be shown by the tip moving forward.

The alternative method is to add extra weight to the feeder until it is well anchored and will not move easily. You then rely on the fish hooking itself against the weight of the feeder as it moves off with the bait. Both methods can work well, though the extra weight required for the second method can lead to a lot of disturbance if the feeder lands in shallow water; stronger hooklengths are also wise with this method to avoid violent bites breaking them against the weight of the feeder.

### Types of Feeder and Tail Length

When chub are the main target species I usually use a block-end feeder, with maggots. On occasion casters are a better bait, and if this is the case I would use them in an open-end feeder; mix them with crushed hemp instead of groundbait to keep them in the feeder until it lands.

The size of the feeder will vary with the head of fish present and the target weight required. However, the ability of chub to consume large quantities of food has already been mentioned, and this means that the feeder tends to be of at least medium size. The main exception is on heavily feeder-fished venues where chub have become wary of them: in these situations a smaller, more discreet model can be more productive.

Tail length will vary dramatically from venue to venue. On some waters the fish dive straight in on top of the feeder and fight for the bait. If that is the case a short tail is likely to succeed by keeping the hookbait close to the feeder and, consequently, close to the feeding fish.

On other venues longer tails are far more successful, where the fish are either wise to feeders and keep a cautious distance from them, or take the bait as it falls. If they are taking the falling bait it will often pay to enlarge the holes in the feeder, so that a lot of the maggots escape on the way down; then use a tail of 4ft (1.2m) or more in length so that the fish have plenty of opportunity to grab the hookbait before it hits bottom. This 'on the drop' method usually requires frequent casting for maximum success. Most other feeder fishing also means regular casting at the start of a session to get plenty of bait down; then later in the session, leaving the bait in position for five minutes at a time will often be the most productive approach.

If I am in doubt at the start of a session as to whether a long or short tail will be best, I usually compromise by starting with one of 2–2½ft (60–75cm) and then make it longer or shorter according to the response of the fish.

### Landing the Fish

Chub have strong, leathery mouths, which offer good hook holds, so there is only a very limited problem with small hooks pulling out. With this in mind I am happy to scale down to a size 22 hook if it is necessary to attract bites; though I should add that if I am using a lot of lead on the feeder a size 20 or even 18 would be a wiser choice, because of the extra pressure put on the hook by a heavy feeder swinging around close to it. These hook sizes would be for maggot fishing; for casters I would usually settle for a size 18.

If the main catching area is going to be close to far-bank cover, I would suggest that you start your session by fishing short of it. By beginning to fish several yards away, you can usually draw fish out and catch them without disturbing the main shoal. Any fish which are scared will move back to the far bank and later in the match you can follow them over, if necessary, and usually catch heavier. If you start your session by fishing tight to the far bank and scare the shoal, they are most likely to move sideways into neighbouring pegs where you cannot get at them! This is of particular importance in clear water, where fish can see what is going on. In coloured water they feel secure, so are often happy to stay well out from the bank.

As with most feeder fishing, casting accuracy is very important, particularly in coloured water, where the fish cannot see the feed if it is any distance from them. Once they do find your feed, your hook must also be there, not five yards away because you miscast.

When you hook chub be aware that they play dirty and go for snags. So if you are hooking them next to far-bank tree roots, boulders, or other obstacles, I would suggest that you do not let them run off. They have not quite got the same power or size as carp or barbel and you can usually hold them. Watch out as well when you get them close to the near bank, if it features any weed-beds or other snags; many a chub has been lost on the nearside this way. I try not to bring them in too quickly, so that they are tired by the time they arrive: then, if they do dive for cover, I give them some stick and bring them quickly to the surface. Once you get them to the surface they usually open their mouths; when they have done this, keep them moving towards the net and they will rarely go down again.

This method is suitable for other species as well as chub. Dace are a common alternative target, as are silver bream, which are surprisingly common in some of our rivers, but are often incorrectly identified as small common bream (skimmers) or roach/bream hybrids. Both dace and silver bream are comparatively quick-biting and, at times, require a counting technique between strikes, similar to the float method which I described for dace in Chapter 3.

## CARP

Another use for the feeder is on lakes which contain a decent head of carp. I have already dealt with catching carp on the float, but sometimes they insist on feeding further out, particularly around islands, which seem to attract them like a magnet.

The rods, reel lines and shock leaders which I use for carp are the same as those used for chub. But the hooks and hooklengths are likely to be stronger, because of the extra size and power of the fish. My normal hook when feeder fishing for carp is a Drennan Superspade, size 18, which will be tied to a standard line of at least 2lb breaking strain. The tail (hooklength) will nearly always be at least 4ft (1.2m) long:

when a shoal of feeding carp move in they are usually big enough to cause a lot of disturbance. The long tail allows the hookbait to be swirled around in the same manner as the loose maggots from the feeder, which seems to attract more bites.

Once carp are in the peg the rod tip is likely to show the activity, as the fish bump into the line. Do not strike at these smaller movements, but wait for definite bites. If you find that the ends of the maggots are chewed after taps on the tip I would suspect small fish rather than carp. Once carp move in the small fish are usually pushed out.

Often, the biggest problem is to get the carp feeding to begin with; this can take some time and usually involves heavy feeding to spark them off. This heavy feeding can be attempted by regular casting of a big feeder; carp usually accept groundbait, however, so why not take advantage of this and use a catapult to feed balls of it to attract them.

This groundbait will need to be sticky enough to hold a lot of feed. If I wanted to catch a big weight I would have at least 4pt of casters plus 4pt of hemp seed with me to feed in groundbait. I might not use them all, but on a big-weight day they could be necessary.

I would feed several egg-sized balls of groundbait at the start and then top them up at regular intervals. If you are going to be fishing at very long range, practise feeding by catapult if you are not used to it. Anyone can fire loose maggots 20yd (18m); firing balls of groundbait 60yd (55m) or more, with accuracy, is not so simple. You may find your catapult is not up to the job, or that your groundbait does not hold together.

The feeder will be on the large size, to get plenty of bait into the peg, and is likely to be a block-end type filled with maggots. On some waters an open-end feeder with groundbait can be better.

Even with heavy feeding it can take some time for carp to arrive. When I won the NFA knock-out cup final at Arrow Valley Lake, Redditch in 1992, I only caught one fish in the first hour, but went on to finish with thirteen for 51lb 9½oz. A couple of weeks later I returned with members of the press to catch some carp for a feature, and it took me two hours to get a bite. Once I caught the first, six more followed in the next six casts. That day I went on to finish with thirteen again for around 60lb, with the biggest individual fish around the 10lb mark.

So you need to have patience at this game, although you can see how few fish can be required! It is not a speed game, and one or two fish per hour can give you a huge weight. So do not rush, particularly when you hook them. Play them firmly, without trying to drag them in (unless snags make this necessary), and make sure of landing them. I have witnessed impatient anglers trying to force the carp to the net before they were ready and consequently losing fish after fish in open, snag-free water. If they had kept calm, and been sensible, they could have placed huge weights on the scales.

Maggots are my most commonly used hookbait when feeder fishing for carp: two or three are about right on the size 18 hook. Floating maggots can help offset the weight of the hook.

## STILLWATER BREAM

There are an awful lot of still waters throughout the country, where various sizes of bream are likely to be regular match winners. On these venues the feeder is often the most effective method to catch them. Bigger bream in particular tend to stay away from the bank, unless there is deep water close in, and usually pick up their food from the bottom – where the feeder can easily place it.

### Tackle

When it comes to tackle, most items can be scaled down from that used for carp fishing. Bream are nowhere near as powerful as carp, so the rod used will be softer, and balanced

*A big bream puts a healthy bend in the quivertip rod.*

main line. At the other extreme, I would consider using a $1\frac{1}{2}$lb line for smaller fish at short range.

As with my float-fishing reel lines, all of my feeder fishing reel lines are standard lines, rather than the extra fine co-polymer lines. Most standard lines break at a higher strain than stated in the spool (so a 2lb main line will actually break at $2\frac{1}{2}$lb, or more), while most co-polymers break at their stated strength. This needs to be kept in mind if you switch to co-polymers; for example, the standard 1lb line which I use for smaller bream, will have an almost identical breaking strain to the $1\frac{1}{2}$lb co-polymer which I also use for the same-size fish! Yet the $1\frac{1}{2}$lb co-polymer will have a smaller diameter. The only reason that I do not use co-polymers for everything is that I am still suspicious about their durability when exposed to extra wear, or sudden shock, such as a heavy feeder and a big fish at opposite ends of the hooklength. Having stated my reservations I should also point out that, apart from heavy feeder fishing, virtually all of my hooks are tied to co-polymer lines, which would not be the case if they were letting me down.

The terminal tackle is fitted with my usual fixed paternoster set-up, with the feeder attached to the end of the main line and the hooklength coming off it about 10in (25cm) above the feeder. The hooklength/tail will be in its usual two parts, with a total length of $3–3\frac{1}{2}$ft (90–105cm) to start with. If the bait was being chewed without a bite registering, I would shorten this distance.

Bream like groundbait, so an open-end feeder is the best to use. The size which I use most often is $1\frac{1}{2}$in (4cm) long and 1in (2.5m) wide, though on low-weight days this might be changed to a smaller one. To attach them to the main line I usually slide a small loop of 3lb or 4lb line under one end of the lead strip, making sure that the knot in the loop is hidden under the lead, and then tie the main line directly to this.

If I am fishing at a comfortable range I often cut down the size of the lead strip; this makes

with lighter hooklengths and smaller hooks. If the fishing has to be carried out at extremely long range, a stiff rod will still be needed to get the distance. But for short- or moderate-range work a soft rod will help prevent unnecessary fish losses during playing.

For large bream, of about 3lb upwards, I like to try to get away with a standard $1\frac{1}{2}$lb line for the hooklength, tying it to a reasonably strong hook, usually a Kamasan B520. For smaller fish I am most likely to use a standard 1lb hooklength, or a $1\frac{1}{2}$lb co-polymer version if I can use very little lead on the feeder (as I have said, I do not like co-polymer lines when I am using heavy feeders). These lighter hooklengths will be tied to finer hooks; a Drennan Carbon Caster would be my current choice.

For casting up to moderate ranges I would use a 2lb main line. This would not be strong enough for long-range work, so I would then use either a shock leader or switch to a 3lb it land with slightly less splash and also puts less strain on the hookhold/hooklength when a fish is being played. Obviously more lead will be required to fish at long range; this is especially true in windy conditions, because accuracy is very important and a light feeder is more likely to be blown off course.

## Identifying Bites

Having cast your feeder to the correct spot, it is important that you can see the bites. Quivertips need to be soft and also reasonably long. The bites are likely to be slower, and more gentle pulls than the violent bites of carp or chub. If the fish feels resistance it is likely to drop the bait, particularly the smaller, skimmer-size fish. If a lot of fish are present you will often encounter line bites, where the tip moves around as members of the shoal bump into the line. When this is happening it often pays to wait for an extra second or two before striking to make sure that you have got a proper bite. Most line bites will pull the tip forward then suddenly let it drop back to its original position as the fish clears the line.

Striking at line bites both wastes time and risks disturbing the shoal, as your feeder is pulled through them on the strike. It is better to use a long soft tip, which the fish will probably not feel, while you delay the strike slightly. Some anglers still prefer a swingtip instead of a soft quivertip, but I have not used one for some years.

To help you pick out line bites from proper ones more easily, I would suggest trying something which I resorted to many years ago. I was practising on the Gloucester Canal when I started to get loads of movements on the tip but very few fish. Eventually I removed my hook and carried on fishing with just the feeder on the line. By watching the indications on the tip I became much more proficient at distinguishing line bites: there was never any doubt as to whether or not the movement was a bite, when I was fishing with no hook!

Another point to bear in mind if you start getting lots of line bites but no fish, is that the fish might be hitting the line some distance short of the feeder. Casting shorter may be worthwhile if the problem continues.

Bear in mind that bream bites do not necessarily move the tip very far. On some days, particularly when the water is cold, the bites might only pull the tip forward ½in (1cm) or less. The possibility that you will need to spot small movements means that it is wise to keep the rod tip close to the water, so that very little line is exposed to the wind. I also sit with the rod butt across my leg in such a way that I can both look straight down the rod – so that I am in the best possible position to see bites – and hold it, so that I can react to a bite without fumbling to grab it. I try to hold the rod for all of my legering, with the one notable exception of carp on days when I am waiting for the rod almost to go in.

As well as using my leg as a back rod-rest I also use two other rests to keep the rod tip as still as possible. Typically, one is close to the tip and the other half-way along the rod. Supporting the rod in three places is extremely effective for eliminating tip vibration, a problem which tends to occur in soft rods, particularly on windy days. The rests should be positioned in such a way that the rod is almost parallel to the bank, so that the line comes away from the tip at something close to 90 degrees.

## Feeding the Bream

The feed I put into the feeder for bream varies, but there are three main variations. For smaller sizes of fish, squatts are my number one feed. I tend to add a few samples of the other maggots which I intend to try on the hook, but nothing else. The hookbait is varied: I use various colours of shop-bought maggots; gozzers, extra-soft home-bred maggots; pinkies; squatts, and various combinations of these.

Squatts will also attract bigger fish, but casters become a better choice when quality fish are the quarry. I feed them in conjunction with a sprinkling of pinkies, which help break up the groundbait and also get the fish interested in maggots on the hook. The hookbait is likely to be one or two casters, one or two red maggots, pinkies, redworms, or various combinations. If fishing a water where the fish are known to respond well to worms, I will consider chopping some up and adding them to the feed.

The third main feed variation is used on venues where the fish respond well to bloodworms and jokers. When this is the case, packing bloodworms or jokers into the feeder and fishing bunches of bloodworms on the hook can be deadly. Other baits which work well in conjunction with this feed include red maggots and redworms.

One other feeder variation which has won me quite a lot of money in the past, is to use a small block-end feeder full of squatts. This would usually be used in comparatively clear water, if the fish seemed to be backing away from groundbait. It can also be very useful if the skimmers are mixed in with other species which are not so keen on groundbait – possibly roach and eels. Occasional soft balls of groundbait introduced by catapult, will often help to attract fish to the feeder in the early stages of the match without scaring them.

The hooks used for my stillwater bream fishing usually range between 24s and 18s. The larger sizes will be for redworms, casters and bunches of bloodworms, while the smaller sizes will be for the various maggots. Size 24s might sound a bit small, and I do not usually set out after large bream with them, but on hard days they can be useful.

When it comes to mixing up the groundbait which is going to be used in an open-end feeder, have a testing session if you are not used to doing it. The groundbait needs to disintegrate fast once in the water, so that if bites come quickly you will not be playing fish with feed still in the feeder. If this happens you will be spreading groundbait over a wide area, as it gradually comes out whilst you reel in; this is an excellent way to split your shoal of fish. To make the groundbait leave the feeder quickly, I suggest mixing it on the dry side. To test your

mix simply drop the feeder into the edge of the water you are fishing and lift it out at intervals to see how quickly the groundbait leaves it. Alternatively test it at home in a bucket.

Sometimes it can pay to mix the groundbait so dry that it comes out almost as soon as the feeder hits the water. This is a technique which I use to catch bream on the drop, especially in hot weather. If the fish are feeding in this manner you will also need to lengthen the tail/hooklength to 5–6ft (1.5–1.8m), so that the hookbait drops very slowly in amongst the contents of the feeder. Tails of this length used to be particularly deadly in the Exeter Canal when many 1lb-size fish were present.

It is possible to feed quantities of groundbait at the start of a session, when bream fishing with a feeder. It can be difficult to decide when to do this, and there is plenty of scope for going wrong. On most venues I will settle for several quick casts with the feeder to get some bait in the right place. Sometimes I will speed this process up by introducing two or three small balls by catapult, which is usually pretty safe. It is larger quantities that can kill the peg if used at the wrong time or on the wrong venue.

If the venue holds a large head of bream which are likely to feed (which usually means warm weather), I will consider using larger quantities, particularly if the water is highly coloured. By large quantities I mean around six balls, the size of small oranges. I would very rarely use more than this at the start of a session when feeder fishing.

I have seen huge quantities used successfully. On the Huntspill in Somerset, it used to be fashionable to introduce huge quantities at the start: some anglers fired out groundbait continuously for the first half-hour of an event. This approach did win matches, but it was also a good way to sit five hours without a bite. Most Huntspill competitors are now far more restrained with their feeding.

## Casting and Playing

Accuracy when feeder fishing for bream is

*Launching a feeder during a long-range session.*

you after a minute or so. This should leave the groundbait next to the hookbait and help to attract bites in hard-fished waters where the fish are scared of feeders. How far you pull the feeder will be determined by the length of the tail you are using.

Playing bream is certainly easier than playing many other species. They do not go for snags, and if they do snag you it will be accidental. If this does happen, do not keep pulling: put the rod down so that the line goes slack, and they will often swim back out. I use this tactic on all species if they go solid on me.

Most bream also lack the power of other species. Occasionally you might encounter a shoal which have been on a weight-training course, but in general they will give in quite quickly to moderate pressure. One word of warning. Smaller sizes of bream have notoriously soft mouths, so do not try to put too much pressure on them to haul them in quickly: your losses are likely to increase.

essential; on still waters it tends to be more difficult to achieve than it is with the chub or carp fishing that we have covered. Chub often give you a far bank as a distance marker, while the best carp pegs often give you an island; stillwater bream often provide nothing but wide expanses of open water to aim at. Accuracy can become a major problem.

To make sure that you are casting in exactly the same direction every time, start by picking out a far-bank marker to aim at; anything will do as long as it is not going to move.

Judging distance is slightly more awkward. The best method is to fix the line in such a manner that you cannot overcast. Most reels incorporate a line clip which can be used for this purpose; on others, an elastic band placed on the spool after you have first cast to the appropriate spot, will do the same.

Once I have successfully cast the feeder to the correct spot, I usually leave it in position, so that the hookbait is close to it. The main alternative is to pull the feeder back towards

*A roach/bream hybrid is landed on a feeder rig from Worsborough Reservoir, Barnsley.*

# RIVER BREAM

If I am trying to catch river bream with a feeder, it will nearly always be large or at least decent-sized fish I am after. The smaller ones are more likely to be caught efficiently with a float. With this in mind the feeder will nearly always contain casters, and a sprinkling of pinkies, rather than squatts or bloodworms.

If the flow is not particularly fast, I will usually fish with the rod positioned low to the water, in the same way that I would on a lake. The quivertip will usually need to be slightly stiffer though, as a really sensitive tip, which is bent double by the current, will be of little use. With this in mind, it is wise to choose leger rods which either feature a range of push-in tips or have separate top sections, each of which have different built-in quivertips.

My reel line for river bream is nearly always 3lb and the hooklengths rarely drop below a standard 1½lb line. The hooks are reasonably strong, to balance with the hooklengths, and are usually fished on tails of 2½–3ft (75–90cm) in length. The feeders themselves will be the same size as the ones used on still waters.

Like their stillwater cousins, river bream tend to stay in deep water (though hot summer weather can change this), so you are unlikely to fish for them tight to the far bank. They are more likely to be somewhere between mid-river and the base of the far shelf, that is, the spot where the bottom levels off, after dropping from the far side. If in doubt, two-thirds of the way across is usually the safest bet.

Unless you are on an exceptionally wide river, accuracy is usually much easier to achieve than on still water. Even when fishing well away from the far bank, it can usually be used as a guide to gauge the range. I still use a far-bank marker as well.

River bream tend to live in shoals which stay in the same pegs year after year. Because of this, it is very unusual for me to introduce any groundbait, by hand or catapult. If I am fishing for them it is because they are known to live in

the peg which I have drawn, and I have no desire to risk scaring them. I much prefer to keep on quietly casting the feeder to the same spot until I persuade them to feed.

### Fishing in Rain-Swollen Rivers

One situation which will see the bream feed over a much wider area, is when the river is carrying extra colour and pace, because of rain. (I am talking about sensible quantities of extra water, not unfishable, raging torrents.) Extra colour seems to provoke the bream into both feeding and roaming over much larger areas of river. With this in mind, I will sometimes fish for bream purely on the strength of the water conditions, even in pegs where they have never been caught.

Tactics have to be altered slightly. The rod needs to be fished with the tip well up in the air, to keep the line off of the water, in the manner that I described for chub (*see* page 74). Extra lead will also have to be added to the feeder to make sure that it holds bottom. With open-end feeders I simply add lead strips next to the one supplied with the feeder. My supply of lead strips comes from broken feeders; if the plastic cracks, I always remove the lead strip before disposing of the plastic.

To help the feeder hold bottom in faster water I would suggest letting out some slack line after the feeder has hit the river bed. I find that a couple of yards of extra line help to reduce the tension between rod tip and feeder, so that less lead is required to hold bottom. With this method I will virtually always be fishing right in front of me, rather than casting down the peg.

In coloured water, worms are likely to become a major force in the hookbait department. In clearer rivers I find that casters or red maggots are usually better, but if I am not catching I am always keen to experiment. Bream can be very fussy when it comes to what bait they take.

As flows get stronger I would also suggest stepping up the strength of your hooklengths.

Bream might not be particularly hard fighters, but they are big fish that can be very awkward to land if they turn sideways in strong currents. Trying to hold 4lb or 5lb of bream, on the end of a 1½lb hooklength, with the current pushing it downstream, will certainly make your heart beat faster. With this in mind I need little encouragement to move up to a 2lb hooklength in strong flows.

Finally, note that bream can be notoriously slow to respond, so do not give up too soon – many a bream match has been won in the last hour or two.

## BARBEL

Barbel could be described as the river version of carp: they are large, very powerful, and greedy. With this in mind, the tackle needs to be of similar strength to that which I have already described for carp.

When feeder fishing for barbel I will use very strong hooks, Superspades in my case, tied to hooklengths of at least 2lb line. In some situations this will need to be stepped up to something considerably stronger.

A good example occurred some years ago when I fished at Bewdley, on the Severn, for the first time. The peg which I drew was very shallow, which is where the barbel like to live, but also full of streamer weed. This weed could be clearly seen and covered most of my peg. The only reasonably sized clear area was towards the middle of the river. I decided to cast to this hole in the weed, using 2lb hooklengths which I considered to be like rope. I had never encountered a situation where it was not up to the job and, at the time, I did not carry hooks tied to anything stronger. I did not have a good day.

I landed the first barbel that I hooked, a fish of about 3lb; but after that I landed only one more. Each time I hooked a fish it swam straight into a weed-bed. If I persuaded it to come out it would then swim into another. I lost a number of fish because the line, which

*This barbel weighed 7lb 13oz and was enough to place the author second in the competition on the Severn at Shrewsbury, in March 1993. It fell to a feeder full of maggots.*

would have been strong enough in fairly open water, was not up to the job in snaggy situations.

I learned my lesson and I now carry strong hooks tied to both 3lb and 4lb line: I do not intend to be beaten by weed-beds, or other snags, again.

Bear in mind that the rest of your tackle will need to be stepped up to deal with these exceptional circumstances. The rod will need to be very powerful and the reel line will also have to be increased. Since 4lb hooklengths, tied to 3lb main line does not sound right to me, I carry a spool filled with 5lb line.

Barbel tend to respond to a lot of feed, but they are not very keen on groundbait. When using maggots I use a decent- to large-sized block-end feeder. This same feeder, with the holes greatly enlarged, can also be used when fishing with hemp and casters, particularly in fast shallow water, where the current is strong enough to wash the feed out of the feeder. The alternative method is to use an open-end feeder and use some crushed hemp to hold the hemp and casters in the feeder.

What you are doing is really just a scaled-up version of chub fishing; the same principle applies of getting lots of feed down quickly at the start of a session to attract the fish. And as with chub or carp, the bites tend to be positive: there is usually little room for doubt when a fish has picked up the bait.

As with other species, it is a wise move to scale down the feed when fishing in cold water, which tends to make the fish less active.

Barbel are not always found in their favourite fast, shallow swims. On some rivers they can be match winners in much deeper, steadier water. The lower reaches of the River Severn, around or below Worcester, are excellent examples of this. The fish here tend to be less numerous, but their size makes up for this. Double-figure fish in matches are very possible!

They can be caught at any point from near bank to far bank. I would suggest picking a spot, then just making sure that you fish it accurately. These fish do not usually look for snags, but their habit of hugging the bottom can make them difficult to land, simply because that is where the snags will be. The best advice that I can offer is to slacken the line as soon as the fish goes solid. If you continue to pull, it will almost certainly break you; if you slacken off, however, it will often swim back out.

## ROACH

Feeder fishing is not the ideal way to catch shy-biting, suspicious roach, but there are times when it is the best option available. This usually means in a river which is carrying some extra water, pushing it through slightly too fast for the float. If the event is likely to be a low-weight affair, roach can still be a practical target.

Rarely will many roach fall to a large feeder. They can be over-fed and the sight of a large feeder also seems to frighten them; a small block-end version is far more likely to be successful.

Hooks for this type of fishing are likely to be 22s for maggots; Drennan Carbon Casters or Kamasan B530s are my current choices. These are tied to either a standard 1lb line or 0.09mm (1½lb) or 0.105mm (2lb) co-polymer. The main line will be 1½lb or possibly 2lb. These lighter lines can be used because of the small feeder, which will often not need to carry much lead.

Accuracy is, once again, essential. You will not be feeding much bait, so you do not want to spread it out. Hooklengths will vary wildly in length, so find the best for the day. Sometimes the fish will feed close to the feeder, but on others they will back off and a 4ft (1.2m) tail can be best. The method can, of course, also produce other species, but roach are usually my main target when I fish like this.

If I am fishing fairly close to the near bank, up to a couple of rod lengths out, I will usually cast down my peg and then position the rod so that it is stuck straight out in front of me. The quivertip will be as fine as I can get away with.

If fishing further out, in flowing water, it is likely that I will have to resort to the rod-up-in-the-air technique, looking for drop-back bites, and use a stiffer tip. Extra lead will almost certainly need to be added to the feeder if you are fishing like this, as most small sizes are supplied with very little attached.

In slow-moving waters I tend to use a feeder only if they are out of loosefeed range. Usually, this still means using a small block-end feeder; if small roach are the target, however, a small open-end feeder, filled with groundbait and a sprinkling of pinkies, can be better. Even so, on slow-moving waters, legering without a feeder is far more likely to catch roach.

### Straight-Lead Fishing

Straight-lead fishing (that is legering without a

*This big roach fell to leger tactics.*

feeder) is a method which can present the bait in a very natural way to fish which would be scared by feeders. In my experience that is most likely to mean roach.

Straight-lead fishing usually comes into play in situations where you are fishing past pole range and the bait needs to fall slowly to the bottom and then lie there. In completely still water a waggler can achieve this, but in slow-moving water a point will be reached where it cannot.

Roach fishing on the Gloucester Canal in winter is an excellent example of this. The canal can tow in either direction, fast enough to make keeping a float still impossible. A second example, from my local circuit, is the lower Warwickshire Avon around Eckington; here the deep slow-moving water keeps a float moving, while the roach often demand a bait which stays put once it has hit bottom.

The tackle used when attempting this style of fishing needs to be kept as delicate as possible, and the weight needs to be kept small. A

¼oz non-toxic bomb is often enough. Alternatively several AAA shot can be used; this makes adding or subtracting weight an easy task, and the shot tends to fall quite slowly through the water compared to the streamlined bomb. There may therefore be slightly less chance of scaring the fish.

Hooks should be kept small, 24s or 22s and should be made of fine wire. These are usually tied to a 0.07mm (1lb) co-polymer hooklength, while the main line is usually 1½lb, as there are no heavy feeders to endanger light lines.

The hooklength is usually attached at least 10in (25cm) from the weight and is generally about 4ft (1.2m) long, to give the fish plenty of chance to grab the bait as it drops. In highly coloured water this length can be shortened, as the fish cannot see the bait falling.

The rod that you use is very important. It needs to be quite soft-actioned, to make playing fish on light tackle easy, and the tips need to be sensitive enough to show delicate bites. Without a really fine tip you are likely to suffer from fish feeling resistance and dropping the bait.

When it comes to feeding, bear in mind that roach can be over-fed. They will accept plenty of bait on some occasions, but if in doubt feed small quantities on a regular basis. Many a winter roach match has been won with less than half a pint of feed.

In situations where the fish are grabbing the bait as it falls, I will endeavour to get my hookbait falling in amongst the loosefeed. In deep water this often means feeding before you reel in to recast.

Once the hookbait is in the water there are two basic variations of presentation that I use. The first involves casting to the far side of the feed area: the bait is allowed to fall, then, if no bite materializes within thirty seconds, or maybe a minute, I pull the terminal tackle towards me 2–3ft (60–90cm). I then repeat the process until I have pulled the hookbait across the whole of the baited area.

Moving the hookbait short distances in this way seems to provoke fish into grabbing it, and also covers a wide area, putting the bait in front of several potential takers. Each cast can be made to a different section of the baited area, until it has all been covered; then you can return to the first spot you tried and start working the area again.

This twitching, or lifting, technique has caught me big match weights of roach from both the Gloucester Canal and the Warwickshire Avon on a fairly regular basis, and works just as well on other similar waters around the country. In the past I also used it in conjunction with groundbait for my bream fishing: but these days it tends to be less effective for them than a feeder.

There are days, though, when roach seem reluctant to accept a bait fished in the manner which I have just described. When this happens I switch to my second method: casting on top of the baited area and leaving the bait in exactly the same place for at least five minutes at a time. I feel that suspicious fish must be inspecting the hookbait for some time before taking it, as bites on this method rarely occur when the bait has only recently settled.

If I use a straight-lead rig these days for bream, chub or other species, it will nearly always be after I have been catching with a feeder, and the fish have stopped biting; I think the feeder may be scaring them.

### The Straight-Lead Rig in Action – Radcot

My first open win was achieved with a straight lead. Obviously it was a major landmark in my career, and one which I have never written about in any detail until now. The year was 1975, the month was December, and the venue was Radcot on the upper Thames.

To say that the day was cold would be an understatement. Several anglers failed to make it to the event because of ice on the roads, and I can remember journeying through mile after mile of freezing fog. I was not driving since I was only sixteen, but I had managed to get a lift with an angler from Tetbury, who was starting to fish occasional opens. Eventually we arrived at the draw, along with 130 others. The

event was a Christmas open, so there were plenty of prizes to fish for on top of the pools, which often encourages a lot of anglers to turn out.

The draw put me on the straight, upstream of Radcot bridge. It was a short walk so I had plenty of time to tackle up. Two rods were assembled: a straight-lead rig on a rod with a soft quivertip, and a float rod, armed with a waggler. The straight-lead terminal tackle was comparatively primitive, but turned out to be very effective: it comprised a $\frac{1}{4}$oz Arlesey bomb sliding on the main line and stopped by a split shot. The distance between shot and hook I cannot recall accurately, but it would have been short – probably in the region of 12in (30cm).

The hook was a size 22, which was very small for those days, but I had already worked out that small hooks led to a lot more bites. It was a fine-wire blue version; if memory serves me right it was a Mustad 313.

My bait supply consisted of casters and bronze maggots. On pegs where the far bank looked 'chubby', casters fished in conjunction with the waggler was the tactic to use. However, the far bank of my peg did not look particularly exciting, so legering maggots two-thirds of the way over was my starting tactic. There were also two other reasons why I did not start fishing the far bank waggler: (a) I could not catapult my loosefeed that far, and (b) the weather was so cold that continually exposing my hands to the cold to feed line from the reel was likely to be unbearable.

Eventually it was time to start and I began fishing single and double bronze maggots on the hook, while loosefeeding maggots as far as I could get them. I was not particularly enthusiastic: the peg had had little recent form and the day was likely to be an uncomfortable one, as we were still in the days before 'moon' boots and one-piece thermal suits.

An hour into the event I was still blank. The only movements on the tip had been a couple of small pulls towards the end of the first hour. They were the kind of movements which are often the result of floating rubbish bumping into the line on its way downriver, but each time it happened I could not help looking suspiciously at the pace of the water. This was a very low, very clear, sluggish winter river, which had not seen rain for some weeks. The movements on the tip were just that bit too quick to be caused by the river. Despite the bait being unmarked on each occasion I took the decision to have a go at the next tiny movement.

I started to hold the rod. Up to that point it had been in rests, so that I could try to warm my hands. I concentrated hard, the tip gave a tiny tap, and I struck instantly. I was both surprised and delighted to connect with something, and it was no gudgeon. After a couple of minutes of very gentle playing, by a young angler who was scared to death of losing it, a 10oz roach was in the net.

Was it a fluke? Apparently not, for ten minutes later a 4oz fish joined it – but that was only the start. The third fish had far more power and I can remember starting to shake with a mixture of excitement and fear that I might lose it. But it stayed on and a roach that was easily bigger than any other I had ever caught was eventually landed. A splendid fish which would have weighed in the region of 1lb 4oz to 1lb 8oz.

My gloves were so bulky that I had had to remove them to play the fish properly; as a result my hands were suffering terribly from the cold. I recast, replaced the gloves and hoped that I would not get another bite too quickly so that my hands would have a chance to thaw out. But they were destined to have little rest, for I continued to connect with the tiny taps. Quality roach began to accumulate in the keepnet and I began to sense the possibility of a victory.

The anglers near by could not get bites and the painful cold was getting the better of many of them, so they began to bank-walk. The obvious place for them to stop was behind an angler who was catching, which meant me. It must have been the first time that I had ever fished in front of a crowd, but fortunately it did not put me off and I carried on catching.

The last couple of hours were slower, but I did catch two smallish bream, which would have weighed about 3lb between them. Then it was all over. The scalesman came along and, before weighing the fish, checked them for length, as we were still fishing to size limits in 1975. Bream had to be 12in (30cm) long, and both of mine just passed. Roach had to be 7in (18cm). The majority of mine were well clear of that, but I did have a sprinkling of smaller specimens which had to be returned; I cannot remember how many. That left me with two bream and about fifteen roach to weigh. The only other species which I had contacted was a solitary minnow.

They pulled the scales round to 16lb 4oz, which at the time was my biggest ever match weight. Looking back, I wish that I had asked the scalesman to weigh some of the biggest roach separately, as I am very curious to know just how big some of them were. I suspect that the best must have been around the 1½lb mark. The runner-up weighed in 8lb 12oz of chub, so I was well clear, and I collected £80 (which was an enormous sum in those days) and a turkey as my winnings.

## FLOODED RIVERS

Another situation where feeders can be particularly useful is on rivers which are suffering from the effects of heavy rain. There are times when the rivers rise rapidly and carry all sorts of rubbish which has been washed into them, making most fishing something between tricky and impossible. Under these circumstances, fishing close in with a feeder can be the only option open.

An excellent example of this took place on the Warwickshire Avon, at Eckington, in 1987 during a West Midlands winter league event. The river was in a terrible state and my early attempts to hold a feeder in the middle were frustrated by the sheer quantity of debris which was being carried down the swollen river. Even with several ounces of lead attached to the feeder, it would start rolling as soon as it landed and the line became festooned with weed, grass and other rubbish, which made winding in a major task.

The situation did not appear to hold much promise and was made worse by my peg being on the outside of a bend: this meant I had no steady water on the inside, except for the gap in the marginal weed and grass where the angler would usually stand. Even this area was swirling around, but it was the only place which was even remotely fishable so I had to try it.

My first attempts to fish it were with a float, but the variable current would not let it settle; it was also difficult to put feed in the right place (as it was impossible to judge where it was landing), so I switched to a tiny block-end feeder.

The hook was a size 20, tied to 1½lb line, and was baited with various combinations of maggots and worms. The feeder contained a few pinkies and dabs of groundbait, which would be washed out through the holes and hopefully attract fish by its smell. Looking back now, I suspect that chopping up a few redworms and adding them to the feeder would have been a good move.

I fished with a sensitive, wand-type, leger rod. Accuracy was no problem as I could literally lower the feeder into the same spot every time.

By the end of the match I had caught five eels and a roach for 1lb 8oz. That might not sound very impressive, but it won my section and finished in the frame, in a match fished by 180 anglers, and from a peg which other competitors were laughing at before the start.

The most successful hookbait was a small redworm, with the end nipped off to hopefully release juices which the fish could home in on. I also missed a couple of bites on a lobworm, a bait which can be very useful in flooded conditions. Being such a big bait they are easy for fish to find and do not get hidden by debris as

quickly as smaller baits. If I decide to try one I usually switch to a size 8 hook tied to at least a 2lb line. A smaller hook would be masked by the bait and lighter line would be asking for trouble from big fish in strong currents.

Another memorable feeder result, on a near-flooded river, occurred several years ago in the Bathampton Christmas open: an event which attracts several hundred anglers to the Bristol Avon between Bath and Bristol.

On this occasion my peg was promising, to say the least; I drew just above Kelston weir, and my peg included the start of the lock cutting, which boats use to bypass the weir.

This draw was a slice of luck which still needed to be converted into fish. I set about doing this by casting a small open-end feeder into the mouth of the cutting. A sprinkling of casters and pinkies were mixed up with the groundbait and the choice of hookbait was varied, though, once again, redworms came out on top.

As usual in these conditions, bites were few and far between. After an hour I caught a 1lb bream, which was very promising. Then, during the next hour, I hooked a much bigger one of about 3lb. I brought it safely to the surface and was reaching for the net, when the surface erupted as a monster pike grabbed it! I lost the bream, as the line was bitten through above the feeder.

Later in the event I hooked another 3lb bream, which was not attacked (presumably the pike was still too full from his first meal), and I also added four eels. My weight of 4lb 15 oz put me second in the match, and without the pike's interference I would have won.

In recent seasons a trend has developed to cancel matches on rapidly rising rivers, so the type of tactics which I have described do not see so much use. However, if you should happen to find yourself fishing in these conditions I hope that I have given you one or two ideas to start from.

# 9 COMBINING YOUR METHODS

Now that you are familiar with the various methods which I employ in matches, we can add another dimension to building a successful approach. There is no rule that says that you can only fish one method, or only one part of your swim, so always look to take full advantage of your whole peg, and assemble all rods which might be of use. I touched on this subject earlier (*see* page 10), when I discussed combining pole fishing for roach with feeder fishing for bream on the Gloucester Canal, in order to get the best possible weight from the peg.

Five hours is a very long time and it is difficult to keep a shoal of fish feeding consistently. If they stop biting, why not catch from somewhere else for a while? A move can both add to your haul and allow the original shoal to regain confidence and start feeding again. By skilfully switching your attention between two (or more) different shoals, the amount of time spent catching can increase dramatically.

## VARYING YOUR TACTICS

There are many different combinations which you can consider. They will vary from venue to venue, but I will give you a few ideas here to assist your thinking.

I have already mentioned the pole and feeder approach on the Gloucester Canal in summer. In winter this is more likely to change to pole and straight lead, as roach replace bream as the main target in the deeper water. If bloodworms are used, two pole lines become very likely instead.

Another classic example is the stickfloat and waggler approach on rivers. Usually the stick-

*Action from the 1988 pole fishing championship on the Gloucester Canal.*

float is fished comparatively close in, while the waggler is used at longer range. Swapping between the two works time after time on many rivers. Even if you are fishing with just one method, you can often increase your catch potential by fishing more than one line. For example, if there is a large head of fish present close in on a river, and I decide to use a stickfloat, I will often feed one line tight to any near-bank cover and a second line a couple of rod lengths further out.

On small canals it is fairly normal to start close in and then move over towards the far shelf. If both of these lines stop producing, a third area, tight to the far bank, can also be considered.

On some rivers the far bank can be relied on to produce some early chub to the feeder before it dies. If this is the case I would certainly be feeding up a secondary line of attack for the float. It is, of course, important that you remember to feed up your extra swims before you move to them, so that they already contain feeding fish when you switch.

## MAKING THE MOST OF YOUR PEG

Another principle, which I usually apply, is to start fishing away from your most promising area! If you feed up part of your peg for some time before fishing it, the fish should become very confident, whereas if you catch the first fish to open their mouths, you may well scare off other shoal members who were cautiously watching the early feeders. With this in mind I

often start fishing in a comparatively unproductive area and rely on catching heavily when I switch. Be warned: this can take a lot of nerve if you are not used to doing it.

There are occasions when I would go straight to my main catching area. Short pegging on rivers springs to mind: this is where the angler upstream attempts to catch fish from the top of your peg, so the shoal is disturbed from the start anyway. Tidal rivers also need to be handled with care. The fish often feed at certain points in the tide, so if that point is at the start of your match you had better be fishing in the right place straight away: it is no good switching after the effect of the tide has turned the fish off. If your main catching area needs to be fed by swimfeeder, this also means that you will need to start there: you cannot build up the shoal without feeding it.

Moving backwards and forwards between two or more shoals of fish certainly offers an interesting challenge. The timing is essential. You need to switch as soon as bites slow down:

*It is easy to smile for the camera when you're catching fish like this.*

if you wait too long, blank spells are going to result and your final weight will suffer. I find these careful and continuous decisions one of the most stimulating and enjoyable aspects of match fishing.

There are occasions when I decide to fish in exactly the same spot all day. Usually this means that I am after large fish, which could show at any time, often on a feeder.

Fishing for big bream is probably the best example of this; but even when they appear to be the only reasonable target, there is no harm in feeding some kind of back-up line, as fishing can be incredibly unpredictable.

### Newbridge: The Advantage of a Back-Up Line

For example, at one point in 1992 I was fishing the Bristol Avon at Newbridge. The river had fallen after recent rain, but still retained enough colour to appear to be perfect for bream. My peg had not produced any quantity of roach for several weeks, but was in a well-known bream area. The tactical decision seemed obvious.

I assembled just one rod, armed with an open-end feeder. Only four or five bream might be needed to win: I would fish for them all match. One per hour sounded easy.

The angler below me decided to fish the pole, which I was pleased about, because it meant that I had a chance of drawing bream from his peg to my feeder. That was the theory: in practice everything was somewhat different. The gentleman below me immediately started catching the roach which were not meant to be there, while I failed to catch any bream, which were. Fortunately the feeder did produce roach, including three huge ones of around 1½lb each. These played a rather significant role in my estimated weight of 6lb after two hours.

This was not bad progress, but I could not imagine that I would continue catching roach of that size for the duration of the event. I kept an interested eye on the progress of the pole angler below me, who was still catching small roach.

After just half an hour of the competition I had taken the precaution of feeding maggots close in, on a similar line to the man below, just in case I needed somewhere else to fish. This now looked like a very wise move. Unfortunately I had not set up any tackle to fish this area, so I had to scrabble up the bank and assemble a stickfloat on a running line.

Why not a pole? The answer is simple: the water was over 10ft (3m) deep and quite pacey. I reasoned that I could catch more fish by running a float well down the swim; the pole was too restrictive. My decision was justified when I netted about 6lb of small roach during my first hour on the stickfloat (which bears out what I said about catching best when fish have been fed, but not caught, for some time). The last two hours were harder but I still increased my total weight to 16lb 9oz, enough for another comfortable win.

If I had stuck stubbornly to my original, carefully chosen tactics, I think it is far less likely that I would have won.

## RIG VARIATIONS

Combining your methods can also involve using different rigs to fish in the same place. For example, a waggler down mid-river, catching fish on the drop, might give way to a big stickfloat (if the wind was favourable), to slow the bait down close to the bottom. A straight-lead or feeder rig might also be considered, for the same mid-river line, in order to present a bait dead still on the bottom.

Different methods provide different presentation and different presentation fools different fish.

# 10 BAIT

Good bait is likely to attract extra bites and gives an angler far more confidence, so it is another important factor in an angler's ability to succeed. Here are some of the most commonly used baits and also some of the less regular ones.

## MAGGOTS

### Large Commercial Maggots

The humble, shop-bought, large maggot probably still wins more matches than any other bait. When bought they should be as large and fresh as possible: the size will make them easier to loosefeed if you want to fish at distance, and will also make the hook less obvious. Fresh maggots are usually bigger as they tend to shrink slightly when they get older. They will also start to toughen up as they age. During really cold weather this might be desirable, as very fresh maggots can sometimes 'stretch' with the cold and stop moving. But in general a succulent, fresh bait seems more attractive to the fish.

A bait fridge is essential for keeping maggots for more than a day or two. I refrigerate mine as soon as I can after buying: once they start to warm up they take a long time to cool down again. When you take them to the river bank in hot weather, spread them out as much as possible to keep them from sweating up; a wide bowl placed in the shade is an effective way to achieve this. Alternatively, take along some form of cool box or cool bag, which uses ice-packs and insulation to keep the bait cold.

I keep my maggots in maize meal, which helps to keep them clean and grease-free. They come in maize meal when I buy them and, unless they are exceptionally dirty, I leave them in this until I am on the bank getting ready to fish. At this point I riddle off the old maize and replace it with fresh maize.

Often I also introduce some turmeric to the maggots. This gives the bait a spicy smell which the fish seem to find attractive. There are two occasions when I do not use it. The first is when I am expecting to catch bream, as I have never been convinced that they are very keen on it. The second is on hard-fished waters where turmeric has been used extensively by anglers for a long time. I feel that the fish are likely to become suspicious of the smell if they have fallen for it lots of times, so it might actually have a negative effect. When I do introduce tumeric, it is not in large quantities. One teaspoonful per pint will do.

When it comes to bait colour, I am one of the odd men out. Bronze, often with the addition of a few reds, is probably still the most commonly used colour, though in some areas of the country, the concern about the safety of some dyes has led to white maggots becoming normal. My own preference is for mostly whites, but with other colours mixed in: bronze, red, yellow or anything else available. I use the same principle as when using turmeric on hard-fished waters: if fish have been caught several times on bronze maggots, they are more likely to accept a different colour. My mixture gives me plenty of different colours to experiment with and, if they do want bronze, I have still got them for hookbait.

Some anglers express doubts as to whether different colours can affect catching, but I am

*Loosefeeding on the Gloucester Canal.*

sure that they do. Too often I have experienced days when only one colour was regularly accepted. I can also remember an occasion, some years ago on the Thames, when I was still using bronze maggots with a sprinkling of reds. I landed a large chub, which coughed up loads of maggots, which were nearly all red! It had been picking them out and avoiding the bronze ones.

## Gozzers

The next size down maggots that I use are the extra-soft home-bred version, which are usually known as gozzers.

The success of these maggots, which see most use for bream or skimmers, is down to their softness: they burst so easily that when a wary fish mouths them, it is far less likely to let go.

You cannot buy these in shops; so if you want to obtain them, but are not sure how to, here is the Kim Milsom guide to breeding

maggots (but bear in mind the rest of your family might not share your enthusiasm for breeding maggots in the garden shed).

All sorts of meat can be used for this task. I always use chicken portions, but hearts are also popular. I would advise against anything which is still covered in feathers or fur as it is will make the job of extracting the maggots much messier.

To get blows from the correct type of fly, the meat needs to be fresh, dry and placed in the dark. I find that older meat placed in the light attracts greenbottle flies, which results in pinkies. Flies are reluctant to blow on damp meat – which often applies to defrosted stuff – so dry it first. The meat also needs to be situated somewhere animal-proof. Cats are partial to chicken, so are foxes and dogs, so I place the meat inside my garage, with the door shut: flies can get through the gaps, predators cannot.

Practice will enable you to judge how many eggs can be accommodated by one piece of meat. Too many, and the meat will be gone before the maggots can grow to full size. If I get far too many blows, I often remove three or four, place them on a separate piece of meat, and use that.

Once I have obtained the blows, I wrap the chicken in several sheets of newspaper and place it in a bucket, which has plenty of air holes in the lid. I then leave it in the garage. When choosing a place to leave the meat, make sure that it does not get excessively hot: some garden sheds are capable of frying the chicken in hot summers.

The length of time which the maggots take to grow to full size varies with the temperature. In hot weather three or four days is enough, but five or six days is more normal. I usually remove the maggots in several batches, over a period of a couple of days, so that I have a variety of sizes available for the hook. Once removed from the meat I place the gozzers in damp bran to clean them.

If I want some coloured gozzers I wait until the maggots have hatched; then I remove some and put them on to a separate piece of chicken, which has had cuts made in it filled with the appropriate dye. The resulting maggots will be internally dyed. Make sure that the dye you use is safe to handle. Even with supposedly safe dyes I wear plastic gloves.

## Pinkies

Pinkies are the larvae of the greenbottle fly and can also be bred at home if desired. Personally, I either settle for pinkie-sized gozzers, taken off the feed early, or I buy them from a shop.

It is unusual for me to feed many pinkies during a match, but they are an excellent hook-bait for many species, so I normally carry some. Even when feeding big maggots, double pinkie can be a surprisingly effective change bait.

The standard colour is a faint pink tint, which gives them their name, but I usually carry a mixture which includes red and bright fluorescent pink.

I find pinkies to be the most durable of maggots, and it is not unusual for me to use them even when they are a couple of weeks old, which I would never do with other types.

## Squatts

The smallest of the commonly used maggots are squatts, which are the larvae of the house-fly. Mine are always shop-bought and, despite the fact that they are a tiny maggot, I want them to be as big as possible! This is particularly important if they are going to be loosefed, as slightly bigger squatts can be catapulted more accurately.

If your squatts are very small, but still very fresh (you will be able to see large feed spots in them), it can be possible to grow them on. They will usually attack bread dampened with milk and, once feeding on this, I have occasionally persuaded them to change to meat.

The squatts are mainly used for either small fish or bream. Their size makes them sink very slowly, making them ideal for persuading fish to feed on the drop. If used through a feeder

for bream, they are less likely than other maggots to burrow into the silt, because they tend to be far less active.

They are usually supplied in red or brown sand, which is excellent for keeping them in; but once on the river bank I riddle this off and add either maize meal, if they are for loose-feeding, or a touch of groundbait if they are to be fed in that.

Squatts are the most delicate of the maggots and this needs to be kept in mind when storing them in a fridge. If they are placed too close to the ice box they might die; I always store them on the bottom shelf.

## Hooking Maggots

When hooking maggots of all types, I virtually always stick to the accepted method of nicking them through the thick end. Maggots sink side-ways, so the idea of hooking one through the middle to make it do the same, should work, in theory; but in practice I have not found it to be particularly successful. Another alternative which can sometimes be useful is to partially thread the maggot on to the hook. This can occasionally be a remedy to missed bites, as the fish can take less of the maggot into its mouth before the hook enters as well.

## Transporting Maggots Abroad

If you need to take large quantities of maggots abroad for a fishing trip, the best method is to refrigerate them as cold as possible, then pack them in airtight containers, which should then be placed in cool boxes. Packed in this way, the maggots will survive for several days. Once you have arrived at your destination, they should be spread out and allowed to revive; they will all be stretched and lifeless at first, but a near 100 per cent survival rate is normal.

# CASTERS

Casters are the chrysalis stage of maggots and

have a tendency to catch quality fish. They need to be fresh; old ones that have died stink, so I would not recommend them.

Most tackle shops will supply you with perfectly good casters. But if your local shop does not, or if you want to turn your own from left-over maggots anyway, here are a few guide-lines.

To start with, the best casters will come from reasonably fresh maggots, rather than ones which have been in the fridge for weeks, nor must they have been exposed to too much heat. Once they have suffered in this way, the resulting casters will be long, misshapen, soft ones, which are useless, compared to the compact, crisp-shelled ones which you want.

I usually leave any maggots I am turning in maize meal. I used to transfer them to damp bran, but as long as they are kept cool I find that the maize is fine. To keep them cool, a garage or cellar floor is usually ideal. But if you do not have anywhere suitably cool during extremely hot summers. I would suggest putting them back in the fridge during the hottest part of the day and then taking them out again at night. Alternatively you can try floating their container in cold water during the day to keep their temperature down.

Timing casters, so that they turn as close as possible to when you want to use them, is down to practice. Generally a few odd ones start to turn first, followed by the bulk during the next two days. Once they start turning I would advise riddling them off three times a day. If the gaps between riddling are too long some of the casters will start to float. Any floaters will be the darkest ones; the lighter the colour, the more recently they have turned.

To store the casters without killing them, I put them in plastic bags then store them in the coldest part of the fridge, making sure to leave some air in the bag. Every time I put another batch of casters in the fridge, I open up the earlier bags to give them some more air.

Once on the river bank, I usually wash the casters in a container of water to clean them off before use. Any floating casters are skimmed off and saved for the hook. These are useful in the same way as floating maggots. They counteract the weight of the hook, so that the bait falls at the same speed as the loosefeed.

To hook them I usually bury the hook completely inside the caster. To do this, stick the point through one of the dark 'eyes' at the blunt end, then push the hook on in, turning it as necessary when the bend of the hook enters. If I am not hitting bites I try another method: I start to pull the hook back towards me when it is all but buried, so that the hookpoint comes back out through the side of the caster; this makes it more likely to catch in the mouth of a fish which is not taking the bait particularly confidently.

Because it is normal to at least partially bury the hooks, they are likely to be bigger than those used for maggots.

## BLOODWORMS AND JOKERS

Bloodworms and jokers are the larvae of midges and gnats. In size, a large bloodworm can be almost as big as a matchstick, though two-thirds of that size is far more normal. Jokers are much smaller.

They are a deadly bait for smaller fish in particular, but are very controversial and often banned. The most common reasons for banning are either concern over too many immature fish being caught, or problems with bait availability. I am well aware that in some parts of the country, obtaining a decent supply of these baits is the biggest problem associated with their use; in some areas virtually no shops sell them. They are also very fragile and suffer from the effects of heat, so during hot summers it can be a particularly difficult task to track down a good-quality supply.

Even if the bait is in perfect condition when bought, they need to be carefully looked after if they are not going to be used for several days. For short-term storage, spreading them thinly in a damp newspaper 'package' and keeping them in a cool place will be fine, especially for bloodworms.

*Out goes a cricket-ball size of bait.*

If you wish to store them for longer periods of time, they will need to be kept in well-aerated water. An aquarium fitted with an aerator and filter is ideal. If you use the bait on a regular basis this is a very worthwhile investment, which will soon pay for itself. Alternatively you can put them in a container filled with water, and then set up a hose-pipe to constantly add extra water to them. The new water needs to be a dribble, rather than a rushing torrent – just enough to keep the water in the container fresh. Obviously it will overflow, so this system usually needs to be set up outside! If bloodworms or jokers are already dying when you place them in aerated conditions, however, they are unlikely to recover.

If you do not have the facilities for keeping them in aerated water, you can always prolong their life slightly by placing them in water for an hour or so each day.

## Collecting Bloodworms

If you cannot purchase bloodworms and jokers locally, or if you want to avoid the cost, you can always try and collect your own. Much has been written on this subject, and it is usually made to sound very easy: so it is, if you can find a supply to collect!

The best way to track down ponds is with the aid of an ordnance survey map with a scale which shows up small ponds. Having acquired a map, you then need a lot of spare time.

Bloodworms live in still waters, so each pond or lake needs to be visited in turn. Many will be hopeless – overgrown or dried up. Only a tiny percentage are likely to hold a worthwhile quantity of bloodworms. The type of pond you are looking for needs to be affected by a mild sort of natural pollution; the ideal pond will be one used by cows to drink. While drinking they often urinate or excrete in the water, which causes the type of mild pollution required. Ponds which receive water drained from farmyards are also good prospects.

One of the problems with finding a decent pond is that very few remain which have not already been found by someone else! In many cases, the original finder will have negotiated exclusive rights to the pond. If he has not, the supply will be put in jeopardy should too many people start using it on a regular basis. When vast quantities are removed there is a danger that there will not be sufficient breeding stock left to repopulate the pond, to the desired extent, during the following year.

If a suitable pond is found, the bloodworms will be living in the silt on the bottom of the pond, so obtaining large quantities will nearly always involve wearing chest waders, to get far enough out from the bank. Obviously this can be dangerous, so always feel your way very carefully if you are not totally familiar with the pond. When trying out a new pond, always take a friend along in case you run into difficulties. Apart from the obvious danger of accidentally stepping into deep water, it is also possible to get stuck in thick silt, so wear a buoyancy aid as a sensible precaution.

Once in the pond, you will require a scraper to collect the bloodworms. This consists of a wooden handle fitted with a metal blade, offset from the handle at an angle which allows it to skim through the silt horizontally. My own blade is made from 3cm-wide stainless steel and is approximately 2mm thick. The leading edge of the blade needs to be smoothed down, so that there are no sharp edges to damage the bait. I use a handle which is 6ft (1.8m) long and the blade extends from the end of the handle by about 15in (38cm). Longer blades can be used in ponds which are particularly snag free.

The blade needs to slide smoothly through the silt and then to the surface. Any jolts or sharp changes in direction will result in the bloodworms falling off, so a smooth technique is vital. The bloodworms come up draped over the leading edge and then need to be separated from the silt, weed, leaves and other pond debris, which accompanies them. To do this you need a two-tiered floating riddle.

The top riddle needs to have a mesh which is similar in size to that used for maggots. Mine is made from plastic mesh, bought from a garden centre. The frame is wooden, so that it floats, and it sits neatly inside the wooden frame of the bottom riddle. The mesh of the bottom riddle needs to be very fine. It must not allow any bloodworms to pass through or get stuck in it. All that should pass through is the silt, which will have fallen through the top mesh with the bloodworms.

Nearly all of the assorted debris which was scraped with the bloodworms, should be left on the top riddle. Once the bloodworms have all wriggled through to the gap between the two meshes, the top riddle can be removed and the debris disposed of. The bloodworms should them be in a virtually neat state on the bottom riddle. If too much rubbish has managed to sneak through the top riddle, simply put them through again.

In most ponds there will be times when virtually all of the bloodworms have hatched out, so there is next to nothing to scrape. The time of year can vary from pond to pond, but spring and early summer are most normal, which can cause problems at the start of the season. This should also be kept in mind if you are trying to search out ponds during the close season. If you find a pond which appears to be perfect but produces nothing, do not write it off straight away; try returning at a later date.

Quantities which can be gathered vary wildly. Some ponds are only of use for collecting enough for hookbait, while others produce massive quantities. I used to scrape in one pond where a pint of bloodworms took less than ten minutes to collect. The blade used to come up bright red with bloodworms, three deep, dripping off it. Unfortunately, that particular pond lost its source of pollution and is now a waste of time: to call it a sad loss is something of an understatement.

One extra point to bear in mind when scraping, is that every time you put your foot down, you are crushing bloodworms, so walk where you have just scraped to cause the minimum amount of damage.

### Collecting Jokers

If you want to collect jokers ponds are no good; jokers are found in polluted flowing water. In practice, this means downstream of sewage outfalls, though I understand that changes in the processes/chemicals used in the sewage works are gradually cutting down the percentage of productive outfalls.

Some outfalls are more suitable than others. Those that discharge straight into big rivers are going to be a bit tricky to scrape, unless you are into scuba diving. What you need is a sensibly deep stream, with a flow which allows discharges to settle. The jokers will be mixed in with the various sediments which have been discharged. (The streams in my area tend to be fast and gravel-bottomed, which is no good. Consequently, I buy all the jokers I use.)

If you are able to find a supply of jokers, you can scrape them in much the same way as you would bloodworms, but you might well find a scaled-down, one-handed scraper easier to use in narrow, shallow streams. When jokers are found in dense concentrations they can also

*Using a tip-rod to achieve perfect bait presentation, tight to the far bank, under windy conditions.*

*Netting a skimmer bream from the Kennet and Avon Canal.*

*Fishing the long pole on the Kennet and Avon Canal, near Bradford-on-Avon.*

*An enjoyable net, mostly roach, which fell to a sliding waggler on the Bristol Avon.*

*Carefully unhooking another fish from the Gloucester Canal.*

*The pole being used to fish the canal's boat channel in winter.*

*Feeding while waggler fishing.*

*A pole-caught skimmer bream from the
Gloucester Canal.*

*A chub which fell to waggler-fished maggots at
half depth comes to the net.*

*Action from the Kennet and Avon Canal.*

*A skimmer is eased towards the net on a hot
summer's day.*

*A small but welcome bream from the Bristol Avon.*

*A mixed haul caught on maggots from the Gloucester Canal in winter.*

*Fish-netting action on the Gloucester Canal.*

*Waggler fishing on the Thames at Radcot during the author's time with Shakespeare.*

*Rod-bending action as a big chub dives for cover.*

*Not a cloud in the sky as another fish falls to the sliding waggler on the Bristol Avon.*

be netted. The net must have a mesh which allows silt to pass through; then, when the silt has been washed out, the jokers can be placed on another riddle to get rid of the debris.

Be warned: many productive joker beds are unhygienic, to say the least, since jokers thrive on pollution. Make sure you are well-protected and wear rubber gloves at all times, particularly if you have any cuts on your hands. Also take care when you are wading: shallow streams still tend to have deep holes, which may be hidden by silt deposits. Follow the guide-lines for bloodworm collecting, and take a friend along in case of accidents.

## REDWORMS

I always carry some redworms with me. Usually their presence is an insurance policy in case I draw on a shoal of big bream, or if heavy rain colours up the river, conditions in which they can often be a top bait.

They also see use during the winter on canals where bloodworms are banned. On really difficult days a small redworm will attract perch, ruffe, bream, gudgeon and sometimes roach or other species, while maggots or casters fail.

The feeding technique in these situations is worth a mention. Redworms (or lobworms) are placed in a feeding cup, attached to the end of the pole, and then chopped up with a pair of scissors. The resulting mess of juice and worm segments is then carefully tipped into the appropriate part of the peg, usually in the deep water. If lobworms are used, three or four will be enough to start with; with redworms, I would start with at least a dozen.

The redworm (or section of redworm) on the hook will be fished either just on, or just off, bottom and will be regularly twitched or pulled around the baited area. Perch, in particular, will often grab the bait while it is moving. When bites slow up, the addition of smaller quantities of chopped worm should help to revive them.

Chopped worms are not only a good feed on

hard canal matches, they can work very well on other occasions as well – particularly when pursuing weights of big bream. In this situation, adding large quantities of chopped-up redworms to the groundbait can lead to large hauls, particularly on some of the big-weight foreign venues, such as those in Ireland or Scandinavia.

The worms I use are gathered with the aid of a gardening fork from the muck heaps in a local farmyard. For anyone in a town who needs a decent supply, a wormery which uses household vegetable waste to feed the worms, is worth considering. If you do start one, try to make sure that you stock it with redworms, rather than brandlings, as this yellow-banded species does not seem to be quite as attractive to fish.

## LOBWORMS

Lobworms can catch fish at any time, but for me they have two main uses: first, as feed in canals, for the chopped worm method outlined above, and second, as hookbait in near-flooded rivers, where their size prevents them from being hidden by rubbish, thus making them easier for fish to find. For this purpose I try to avoid the full-grown monster versions, settling instead for half-grown worms, which more fish can get into their mouths.

Lobworms are easy enough to collect providing you have a torch, a mild night, a grassy area and plenty of stealth.

When night-time conditions are suitable, the worms come to the surface and partially leave the ground. Any sign of disturbance causes them to retract back into their holes with surprising speed. But, by treading carefully, it is easy to pick them out with a torch and grab them with your free hand. Once you have got hold of them do not pull too hard or you will be in danger pulling the worm in half. Under steady pressure they will suddenly release their grip and slide out smoothly.

To keep them I usually add some earth to

their container. If you wish to keep them for any length of time, it is important to remove any that are dying, for if one dies the others will soon follow.

One of the biggest problems associated with lobworm fishing is missed bites. The fish tend to pick up the end of the worm and often signal a bite while the hook is not actually in their mouths. The best way to overcome this is often to hook the worm twice. First pass the hook through close to the head and slide that up the line, placing a small shot on the line to stop the head sliding back down. The worm can then be hooked a second time, close to the tail. This method presents the worm in such a way that the hook is far more likely to be taken into the fish's mouth.

## BREAD

If you intend to fish with bread punch, make sure that you are using a type which stays on the hook well: some are much better in this respect than others. Whatever type you end up using remember that freshness is important: once bread starts to dry out, it will be far more difficult to use, so try to buy it the day before it is required. If you do get caught out and it is not as fresh as you would like, try holding it over a steaming kettle to remoisten it, or place it in a microwave oven for a few seconds to achieve the same effect. When it is on the bank with you, keep it in a plastic bag.

The same type of bread which you choose for punch fishing, will also be fine for use as bread-flake on bigger hooks for larger fish. I must admit, however, that this is a bait I rarely use.

## HEMP

I tend to use hemp as feed rather than hook-bait. I know that many people use it on the hook with great effect for roach, but I stick to other baits with no apparent ill-effect on my results.

The species I would most commonly feed hemp for are carp, barbel, eels and small roach. I say small roach because I find that they seem to be attracted by its smell, and can then be easily caught on squatts or maggots. For large roach I rarely feed hemp. I find just feeding the same bait as will be used on the hook more effective. Many times over the years I have caught decent roach by feeding nothing but maggots, while neighbouring anglers have fed hemp and caught much smaller roach on the same maggot hookbait.

The inclusion of eels on the list might well be a surprise to many people, but I have found that the introduction of hemp at the start of a session will often draw eels into a peg more effectively than maggots on their own.

If hemp is used on the hook, it is usually at its most effective in clear water conditions. To put it on the hook, most people push the bend of the hook into the split in the seed; alternatively, it is possible to hook it through the shell. This method will leave the hook far more visible, but the seed will stay on the hook for ages; this method is of most use when the fish are feeding particularly well.

To prepare hemp I place it in a saucepan with water, bring it to the boil, and allow it to simmer for thirty minutes. By this time the seeds will have split to show the white shoot. I would strongly recommend that you use an old, and otherwise disused, saucepan for this job.

Tares are a larger seed bait which are commonly used as a hookbait, in conjunction with hemp. I have caught fish on them in the past, but have not used them for some years now. If you want to try them, cook them in the same way as hemp; possibly adding some bicarbonate of soda to the water, which will darken them to match the hemp.

Other seed baits see very little use in matches. Many, many years ago I caught some fish on stewed wheat in a match! But I am most unlikely ever to use it, or any other off-beat seed baits, again.

## OTHER BAITS

There are a number of other baits that see use in matches, which I have little or nothing to do with, but which are probably worth a brief mention.

One of these is luncheon meat. I have caught chub on lumps of meat on a number of occasions over the years, usually in near-flooded conditions where its size and smell help the fish to find it. On some rivers it sees a lot of use for barbel, in the same coloured conditions, though I have to admit that I have never caught a barbel on it myself.

If you want to fish with meat in such waters, the hook should be a size 10 or bigger, and it is normal to fish it on a straight-lead rig rather than a feeder. The rod and line both need to be on the powerful side, considering the species being sought and the power of the river's flow.

Another species I have caught on luncheon meat is carp. I am occasionally invited to fish a lake which holds a large population of both mirrors and commons, but is also teeming with tiny roach, which grab a maggot within seconds, resulting in hours of frustration. By fishing small pieces of luncheon meat on size 18 or 16 hooks, the tiny roach are eliminated and the carp can be caught in numbers; I have even caught the odd big roach on it! My feed in this situation consists of lots of hemp seed and some chopped luncheon meat. I am sure that this cannot be the only water in the country where this type of situation exists.

Another large bait, used for chub in particular, is cheese paste, which, unlike luncheon meat, is mainly used in clear water. Danish blue, with some bread mixed in to stop it from going too hard in freezing water, is popular on my local upper Thames in winter, where a handful of chub is often likely to win. As with meat, it is nearly always fished with a straight-lead rig and big hooks. I must admit that trying to catch three or four chub on a lump of cheese holds little appeal for me, so I tend to avoid the venue when this method rules.

I once fished a match with boilies, because I was assured that they were definitely the winning bait for the lake's carp population. I caught one bream on them and have not even considered using them in a match since.

Sweetcorn catches loads of fish in pleasure sessions; I cannot recall ever catching on it in a match, though I have seen it work, for bream in particular.

Finally, wasp grubs are a bait which definitely do win matches in this country, though they are banned on many venues, including many in my area. I have never used them, since I have always managed to fight off the urge to try to remove them from nests which are guarded by fast-moving, aggressive insects with the ability to sting. I know you are meant to poison them first, but on the odd occasions when you do not kill them all, they are not likely to be particularly friendly when you start attacking their home.

## GROUNDBAIT

I use a number of different groundbaits, including pure bread in its various forms: brown crumb, white crumb and liquidized. The white crumb and liquidized bread see most use in conjunction with bread-punch hookbait, while the brown crumb is sometimes added to Van Den Eynde groundbaits if I am fishing for bream.

The rest of my groundbaits all come from the Van Den Eynde range, which was so even before my involvement with Van Den Eynde. The ones which I use most often are 'Supercup' and 'Hi-pro specimen', which is now being repackaged as 'Carp'. I also add 'Special' to 'Supercup' if I want a very cloudy mix, for fishing on the drop. In deep and/or fast water, on the other hand, 'Natuur', 'World Champion' and 'Turbo' are all possibles.

Kastaar is an excellent groundbait for bream and, of course, the other mixes in the range have also been carefully developed to catch plenty of fish. The only reason that I do not

*Preparing to groundbait at the start of a pole fishing session.*

use more from the range is that I have settled on a selection which I have found covers all my groundbaiting needs.

It is well worth experimenting on your own waters with the different varieties available.

This is best done by a group of anglers, rather than just one. By all fishing in an identical manner, but using different groundbaits, a pattern will emerge as to which mixes are most successful for various species. It is a great boost to your confidence when you then fish matches knowing that you are using the ideal groundbait for the venue/species concerned.

When mixing groundbait, remember to do it well before the starting time. Groundbait absorbs water over a period of time, rather than instantly, which means that you will probably have to add water several times. Each time you add more, make sure that it is evenly mixed in, so that all the groundbait is of the same consistency.

If the groundbait is to be used to create a cloud effect in the water, it should be mixed either very wet or very dry, while groundbait which is designed to go straight to the bottom should be mixed in between those two extremes. It is a simple matter to test it by squeezing it into a trial ball.

The main species for which I use groundbait are all sizes of bream, gudgeon, carp, tench and small roach. Bigger roach sometimes accept it, as do perch when it is used with bloodworms. All other species will accept it at times, but those listed above are the most useful targets, in my experience.

# 11  READING THE VENUE

The various species of fish which we try to catch do not all like the same water conditions; consequently some knowledge of which species are most likely to feed on a particular day is rather useful. Some species feed best in clear water, others in coloured; it is also worth remembering that coloured water will give fish more confidence to venture close to the near bank.

Fish in clear water tend to be very wary, because they are more visible and therefore an easier target for predators such as pike, mink and herons. They are, of course, also more likely to see anglers, and either back off or stop feeding. They also shoal up more tightly, finding security in numbers, so matches can often be patchier in unusually clear conditions. Weed-beds, overhanging bushes, or similar features are also a big bonus in clear water conditions, as they offer much sought-after cover for the fish.

In clear water fish are more likely to accept a bait off bottom, as they can see it more easily, while in coloured water they tend to grub around on the bottom in search of a meal. If the flow is very fast in coloured water, a leger/feeder rig will help to keep the bait in one place long enough for the fish to find it.

Temperature also affects fish. They are cold-blooded, and consequently become more active in hot weather (though in prolonged periods of extremely hot weather, oxygen levels can fall and the fish do not feed so well). Remember that in freezing-cold winter conditions, fish will be at their most inactive, and cut back the feed accordingly. Generally speaking, in very hot summer conditions, the well-oxygenated shallows are often the most productive areas, while

*Action from Ireland – not the easiest water to read.*

in cold winter weather many fish retreat to the deeper water.

Wind might make fishing more awkward but, in general, it is welcome, since many fish seem to feed more freely in rougher conditions.

Overcast days are also good, particularly in clear water, because dull conditions provide the fish with more cover and therefore more confidence. Overcast days also usually occur during periods of low pressure. For years, some anglers have claimed that fish feed better during times of low pressure, rather than high pressure, but I dismissed the idea. However, of late I have become more convinced that low pressure does have a beneficial effect, and it might not just be coincidence that windy days are another common feature of low-pressure areas!

The most ideal river conditions occur when water is carrying just a touch of extra colour and pace, often when the river drops following floods. The fish will be hungry after fighting the extra current brought about by the floods and, as the river drops, the colour will reach a point where both the clear- and coloured-water loving species all decide to feed.

The same pace and colour as the river rises is not usually so productive. The fish will not have been working up an appetite by fighting a strong flow, and all sorts of bankside rubbish will be carried by the river, making fishing very awkward at times. The extra water may also be cold and, if this is the case, it will almost certainly stop a lot of fish feeding.

I will now run through the various species, and give an indication from my own experience, what types of conditions they prefer to feed in. It will hopefully be a useful guide to readers with limited experience to call on.

Bear in mind that all my guide-lines refer to daytime match conditions. Nearly all of the events which I take part in run from 10 a.m.–3 p.m. or 11 a.m.–4 p.m.; if you fish early-morning or late-evening matches the fish will often be easier to catch, particularly in clear water, when the lack of light gives the fish more confidence to feed.

## ROACH

Roach are happy to live in virtually any speed or depth of water, with the possible exception of very shallow stretches of rivers; this makes them an ideal species to predominate on a match venue, as they are more likely than most other species to be present in a high percentage of pegs.

They feed at their best in water which is coloured to some extent; very clear water usually makes them very cagey. Cold water can also turn them off, with the larger members of the shoal usually being the first to stop feeding.

In times of near-flood conditions, they prefer to live in water which is flowing smoothly in one direction; for example, just around a bend, where much of the current is diverted towards the far bank. As with most other species, they are not keen on heavily boiling water, nor are they particularly enthusiastic about water which is going around in circles, which often happens in areas such as cattle drinks.

## BREAM

Bream show a strong preference for coloured water. Extra colour brought into a river by rain, multiplies the chances of them feeding, and often persuades them to spread out over a longer length of the river. In clearer water the large fish can still be caught, but they are usually shoaled tightly in certain favoured pegs. The smaller, skimmer-sized fish have an unfortunate knack of vanishing completely in clear water.

Larger bream also display a liking for deep water (with the exception of very hot early-season weather) and this usually means that they will be found well away from the banks. On rivers, the areas where they hole up also tend to be relatively wide.

On still waters bream tend to wander over quite large areas, often being influenced by the wind, moving towards the side into which it is blowing. They are not particularly keen on cold water, and in lakes will often stop feeding in the depths of winter. In rivers the flow tends to keep them more active, so they will feed to some extent in colder conditions.

Bream show a distinct preference for rough, windy weather, which seems to stir them into activity.

In summary, mild, windy weather and well-coloured water should have you asking about the size of a venue's bream population.

*Netting a bream on the Gloucester Canal.*

## PERCH

Perch are happy to feed in clear water, probably because they are predatory, and high visibility makes tiny fish easier for them to see and consequently catch. They do also feed in coloured water, but are definitely less enthusiastic.

Their habit of attacking shoals of fry-sized fish means that they will often be found close to weed cover, where fry seek refuge. I would think that most anglers will have witnessed perch chasing tiny fish around the shallow weedy margins of lakes.

Perch are also one of the species which are happy to feed in extremely cold weather. Many a hard winter canal match has been won with a haul of perch on worms or bloodworms, on days when even the roach have refused to play.

Perch can turn up just about anywhere, but most winning weights of them come from lakes or canals. I can think of few occasions when I have seen them dominate a river match.

## DACE

As with perch, dace will happily feed in very cold water. They will also feed in either clear or coloured conditions, though showing a preference for coloured, and are one of the last species to stop feeding as a river rises and colours up.

They do not like still waters, though there is a surprisingly large population in some canals. On rivers they often live in the shallowest pegs available, where the flow will be at its greatest.

## GUDGEON

Gudgeon are considered by many people to be a flowing-river species, but the size of the population in many canals and some lakes, suggests otherwise.

They turn up in all sorts of depths of water, but to catch a substantial weight of them, their size dictates that they need to be located close to the angler. On canals they tend to move up the shelves in coloured water, and head for the deep centre channel as the water clears in the winter. Once in the deep water they tend to shoal more tightly, particularly in the narrow areas next to bridges, but can still be caught despite cold or clarity.

On venues with extensive shallow areas close in, gudgeon will often swim surprisingly close to the bank, in large numbers. The rowing course venue at Holme Pierrepont hosts a thriving gudgeon population; if you set your stall out in the shallow margins, a couple of yards from the bank, it is not unusual for them to grab your hookbait by your feet, when you drop it there before feeding a long pole out. They can be caught in quantity with short whips but, due to the substantial target weights on the venue, these are rarely used. A similar situation used to exist on the Thames at Medley in Oxfordshire, where huge shoals of gudgeon patrolled the shallow margins at such close range that they could sometimes be seen.

*Action from a competition at Holme Pierrepont.*

Gudgeon sometimes win matches on rivers, but more often play a supporting role by adding several pounds to a catch which revolves around larger species. This role is carried out in all conditions, as they are another of those heroic species which continue to feed come floods or freezes.

## RUFFE

Ruffe have similar likes and dislikes to gudgeon, but tend to be prolific in far fewer venues. I cannot think of any lakes which hold a decent population, and they also seem to be completely absent from some rivers. For example, I cannot remember ever seeing one caught from the Bristol Avon.

They are a very unlikely winning species in rivers but, as they continue to feed in the coldest of conditions, they can be of use in very low-weight matches where virtually nothing else feeds. Worms or bloodworms are the baits which should be considered.

On canals they come into their own when the water starts to clear and other species stop feeding: this is when they are most likely to have a major impact on match results.

If they are the main target species, the use of groundbait is usually unwise. Most ruffe populations show a distinct aversion to it and should instead be attracted by chopped worms or jokers, either neat or held together with leam.

## BLEAK

Bleak are usually most active during the hot summer months, when their presence can make them a worthwhile target in matches where the winning weights are modest. Once the frosts arrive, bleak tend to vanish completely from huge lengths of river, or shoal up tightly in a few favoured spots.

Despite the fact that they usually live and feed just under the surface, they still like to have a reasonable depth of water underneath them and do not like venturing into very shallow water. To keep them close enough to build a big weight, some kind of weed cover between angler and fish is also useful, though not essential.

In the same way that bleak can vanish in cold weather, they can also reappear, as if by magic, after heavy rain, when the river colours up (even if it is freezing cold). This is probably when bleak are of most use, as they go on a feeding spree, preferring steady rather than boiling water. The ideal peg is one where partially submerged bankside trees hold a lot of the water back and the fish shoal tightly in the area behind.

Bleak can be safely regarded as a running-water species. They can sometimes materialize from nowhere on some drains and canals when rain colours up the water, but I cannot think of any lakes which hold a population.

## EELS

Eels have similar likes and dislikes to bleak, though they feed on the bottom rather than on the surface. When river conditions become too flooded for virtually all fish, bleak and eels are often the last ones left feeding. In normal river conditions they feed at their best in hot weather, all but vanishing in winter.

The largest populations of eels seem to be found in many of the large drain-type rivers, although most natural flowing rivers also hold them in at least passable numbers. There are exceptions though: for example, I have never yet seen one caught from the Thames. I would also struggle to name any lakes or small canals which hold a population large enough to make a worthwhile target; most lakes seem to hold them, but only as the odd large fish.

In flooded rivers eels will come in close to the bank, but under normal conditions I find that most eels are caught in deep water; nor are they keen to feed if the water is too clear. However, in coloured water and hot weather they provide many good summer-time weights from the large drain-type rivers they prefer.

## CARP

Carp are basically a still or slow-moving water species, which have a strong preference for hot summer weather; but they will also feed, to some extent, in winter.

If many are present and feeding, the venue will almost certainly be coloured, as their size and enthusiasm for digging up the bottom in search of food stirs up the silt, particularly on small, shallow, heavily stocked ponds.

Carp like to cruise around shallow margins, but the bankside activity during a match will often drive them (especially the larger ones) further out, where they will either make use of any convenient islands, or simply head for the middle of the lake, as far away from trouble as they can get.

## TENCH

Tench preferences are very similar to those of carp, with hot weather, still (or at least slow-moving) water, and the presence of margins to swim around, all close to the top of the list. However, as with Carp, they will often be pushed further out from the bank when a match is on. Their feeding habits are also similar to those of carp, in that they often demand large quantities of feed to turn them on.

## BARBEL

A look at the barbel's preferences definitely takes us away from the stillwater species. Barbel like rivers, preferably fast ones.

Small and medium-sized fish often take over any shallow fords which may be available on large rivers, where they become a major species; the bigger ones often lurk in slightly deeper and steadier water. They do not seem to mind being visible in the shallow water, as long as they can keep well away from the bank. This lack of concern also extends to clear water, where they can often be match winners.

They will also continue to feed in highly coloured water; the only water condition which does slow them down dramatically is the cold. They are far less active in the depths of winter.

When they are present in smaller, winding rivers, they seem to like deep undercut banks, and shoal up in these favoured spots.

## CHUB

Chub feed best in water which carries just a tinge of colour. If it becomes heavily coloured they are not at all keen.

As far as temperature is concerned, they are a resilient species and are happy to feed in very cold water. In the heat of summer they also feed, though then often in shallower, well-oxygenated stretches of water.

They also make more use of bankside cover than any other species. Overhanging far-bank bushes or trees are the classic chub pegs and, even if no bankside cover is present, they will often inhabit undercut far banks. Underwater snags (such as sunken trees) are also favoured, and they make good use of these when trying to get away when hooked. They can also be caught on occasions close to near-bank cover, but it needs to be undisturbed – chub are very wary.

On larger rivers, which tend not to have undercut banks, they spread themselves out over quite large areas. On smaller rivers, their liking of features they can hide under can lead to very unfair matches. Though in perfect conditions, where the water carries just a tinge of extra colour, they will roam further.

Although chub are basically a river species, they also account for quite a few wins on canals, usually from far-bank cover again, which here often takes the form of moored boats.

*Action from a match on the Bristol Avon in 1984.*

It is hoped that this very basic guide will be of assistance to comparatively inexperienced match anglers, trying to come to grips with the sport.

It will be especially useful during fluctuating water and temperature conditions. A low, clear river, which is dominated by hauls of chub one week, will be a totally different proposition the next if rain introduces extra colour. Bream, for example, will become a far more reliable target and the chub will all but vanish. Tactics should be altered accordingly. If the river then deteriorates even more, bleak or eels may take over from bream: it is a big help if you make sure that you are fishing for a species which is likely to respond.

# 12  TEAM FISHING

As well as competing in individual competitions, most anglers also like to be involved in team matches. There is something special about sharing a triumph with a group of friends who have all played a part. But, as with the individual events, winning is not easy.

Many anglers fish for just one or two clubs or teams throughout their careers, but I have found myself turning out for many different ones over the years. I have seen action under many different leaders, fished alongside numerous team mates, at all sorts of levels and with varying degrees of success.

Recounting my team fishing experiences and trying to explain the reasons behind the successes and failures, is probably the best way to convey my ideas on how a team can succeed, as well as being of interest to those curious about my career. I began as a team angler in the days when we all had long hair and wore flares.

## THE DOLPHIN ANGLING CLUB

My debut in a proper team event came way back in 1973, when I appeared for the Dolphin Angling Club (from Tetbury), which I had joined in order to fish my local lake. The event concerned was a round of the Stroud and district summer knock-out cup; an event which was usually entered by twenty or more six-man teams from the local clubs. The format was a one-against-one knock-out basis, with each round being decided on total weight over two legs: one home and one away. Apart from the final, every match was a two-hour evening event.

*A crucian carp is netted from Willow Park Lakes.*

I was brought into the team as a reserve, when someone dropped out at the last minute. I cannot remember who we were fishing, but they took us to their choice of venue, which was the Gloucester Canal. I had not quite mastered the canal at that time and my catch weighed in at 1oz; fortunately no one else had mastered it either and I finished second!

The second leg on our club lake was marginally more productive, with the Dolphin team powering through to the next round, aided in a minor way by my 14oz.

For the next round we drew away in the first leg to a club called Stoutshill, who used their carp-filled club lake for home matches. I had fished the place once before and seen a lot of carp caught by anglers using 'dough bobbins' as bite indicators while legering. I decided to do the same.

The carp were not large, but were bigger than anything I was used to, so my tackle was on the strong side: 4lb line, straight through to a size 14 hook. I was not taking any prisoners. Our team won the match, with three carp between us, of which I caught two for 4lb 4oz and took second place. This was a surprise result which we failed to follow up on, as we lost the second leg and went out of the competition.

That, then, was my introduction to team fishing. You will have probably worked out from the lack of fish caught, what kind of standard the team was at. Practice, team plans and information sharing were not features of our team (though, to be fair, information cannot be shared if you have none!)

Nobody had experienced any real success; the club was not used to winning and consequently many of the team members did not even hope to win, let alone expect to. People dropping out at the last minute was a common occurrence, and the team was bonded together so loosely that I rarely knew the names of all the team members.

Over the next few seasons I fished in a number of team events with the club, all of them on a comparatively local basis, often in winter league matches. Our success, teamwise, was a spectacular zero, which echoed our lack of experience (or perhaps ability) and commitment. This lack of commitment exposed itself in subtle little ways, like going to the pub halfway through if you were not catching.

### The 'Youth Team'

The closest I came to team success with the club was in 1978. By that time I was winning lots of club matches and I think this had helped to generate interest from other young anglers in the area. Consequently there were a number of other very keen teenagers, and we decided to enter ourselves in the Stroud knock-out cup.

There was only member of the side older than I, the father of one of the youngsters. His presence was vital: he had a car! This brought our vehicle total for the team up to two, but mine was not much help, being up to the usual standards of a first-time car – bought with little money soon after my passing the driving test.

Our young team was ready to take on all comers. We were full of youthful enthusiasm and all had a genuine desire to do well. At that age you do not realize just how little you really know, so you are not scared of more experienced opposition.

The draw for the first round was made and we found ourselves up against one of the top club teams in the competition, Leonard Stanley, a village situated just outside Stroud. We won the first leg, then lost the second, but won by 1oz overall. We were ecstatic.

We then proceeded to comfortable wins in the following rounds, against weaker opposition. Many of the teams had a 'star' man who they would place wherever he wanted to be (which was allowed by the rules. One team had an odd number and the other even, but it was entirely up to each team whether they then drew or not). We then used to go in for man-to-man marking, which meant that I and our other best angler would see where the opposition's star was fishing, then take the pegs each side of him, so that if he had sat in the best place we were in the best position to cancel his efforts out.

Anyway, our efforts saw us safely through to the semi-final, where we came up against intimidating opposition: a team which was a match group, rather than a club side, called the Falcons.

We were at home in the first leg and decided to take them on at our local club lake. We also decided to take a gamble which would give us an excellent chance of beating what was a far better side. The lake was very weedy and we pegged it out in such a way that one draw would give some excellent weed-free pegs, while the other draw consisted of weeded-up pegs, which would be very difficult to fish. This was not particularly sporting, but well within the rules. We drew the best set of pegs, but the lake switched off totally and most of us blanked, though we did win the match by a very narrow margin. In the second leg we lost narrowly and went out of the competition by very little, I think 1oz.

So we did not win. However, I got a feel for what might be achieved by a team which tried hard and really wanted to win. I had also discovered one of the problems of team fishing which had to be overcome. During a number of matches I spent far too much time looking anxiously up and down the bank, worrying about how the rest of the team were getting on. At the end of the match it would often turn out that they had done better than me, largely because I had forgotten to concentrate on my own fishing!

This is a problem which many people suffer from. It is essential for an angler to learn to concentrate on his own efforts and forget about team mates. The only way in which you can help them is by catching well yourself. I can now shut out concerns about other anglers to such an extent that I often ask bank runners not to tell me how my team is getting on, particularly if I am under pressure; I do not want any form of distraction.

Unfortunately the young team broke up before the following season. Two of the best anglers all but gave the sport up. The names of Julian Arthurs and Gary Hobbs could have been heading for big things within angling. Instead, Gary joined a local rock band, while Julian discovered women and, judging by his quick exit from the match scene, he was pretty enthusiastic about what he discovered!

## LEONARD STANLEY

For the first couple of months of the next season (1979), I did not fish team events. Instead I made the move from fishing mostly club matches, to fishing mostly open matches.

Then, while practising on the Gloucester Canal, I struck up a friendship with one Brian Pollard, who, by sheer chance, happened to be practising on the same day, in the same place. Brian was the star member of the Leonard Stanley team, which we had narrowly beaten the previous summer. I had spoken to him briefly on a number of occasions in the past, but never at length. It turned out that he, too, wanted to move on to the open circuit and we decided that it would be an easier task if we tackled it together. So a friendship formed, which has lasted to this day, and I joined the Leonard Stanley club so that I could fish with them in team events. Apart from Brian, Leonard Stanley already included Chris Jurevicius in their line-up, who was also very good by local standards.

Andrew Jones, who had also been part of the young Tetbury team moved to Leonard Stanley soon after me. Suddenly we had a very strong basis for six-man team events, particularly as many were fished with the rule that only the best four results counted. We were young, learning fast, very enthusiastic and worked together well. That was easily good enough for us to start winning as a unit.

During the early 1980s we carried off the local knock-out cup three times and the Severn Vale shield (which was a local, one-match team event, decided on points) four times. We also ventured slightly further afield and carried off the Avon commercial league on a regular basis; most of those matches were on the Bristol Avon. I remember one year in those matches when I managed five section wins and a third in the six-match series, but was still beaten by Brian who managed five firsts and a second!

We worked hard at what we did, practising when necessary, sharing information and all fishing very strenuously. That was one of the most important factors – when an angler is in a weak team, it is easy for him to give up before the start if he has drawn poorly. If several members of a team have that attitude, they cannot win. In a good team there is self-belief, and everyone knows that if the team fishes to its best ability, they are likely to win. The key anglers in the Leonard Stanley team became extremely reliable – nobody wanted to be responsible for the team losing.

Captaincy was an interesting issue. It was actually difficult to work out who was in charge, as we worked so well together, which is a rare situation. Apart from someone to pay the pools and do the draw, we had no need for one; the organization and motivation was a team effort.

We enjoyed our success and looked forward, in particular, to some of the presentation nights, where the alcohol-fuelled celebrations sometimes bordered on the dangerous. Brian was the worst casualty that we suffered, and he was off work for a fortnight: the damage to his leg was sustained when he crash-landed during a particularly vivid interpretation of the Rolling Stones' 'Jumping Jack Flash'.

As winning became too easy, we looked for bigger team challenges to move on to; it would have been pointless to have carried on winning at the same level. Also, we would have been in danger of discouraging other anglers in the area, who might have given up match fishing if they felt that they had no chance of winning.

## SWINDON ISIS

We (Brian, Chris and I) had already started to fish NFA nationals for another team, Swindon Isis. Nationals are twelve a side, and bigger teams are more difficult to organize and weld into a winning unit. This showed during our time with Isis. The leadership was strong, in the form of Peter Gilbert who still captains them today, and who is always looking to do well. He finally achieved this in 1992, when Isis were runners-up in the NFA first division national.

At the time when I was involved in the Isis team, recruitment of quality anglers was a problem for them, largely because Swindon Talisman were at their peak and could attract the best of the Swindon anglers. Isis were lower down the pecking order and always in danger of losing their best men. As a result of this situation, many members of the Isis team were fairly young and inexperienced, which causes problems in team matches on distant venues; experienced anglers will come to grips with a strange venue far quicker than inexperienced ones.

The first national which I fished with them certainly was on a distant venue, the Leeds and Liverpool Canal. It was the first ever national on the venue, so information was scarce and it was certainly different to anything I had encountered before. Teamwise we finished twenty-third out of seventy-three teams, with me scoring sixty-one points for my 3lb 9oz, which consisted of five small tench and four tiny roach, on pole-fished casters. The pole I used was actually borrowed for the day, as the one which I used on the Gloucester Canal was not long enough to reach the fish on the Leeds and Liverpool.

Later in that same season we fished the NFA south-west regional championships, which was on the Gloucester Canal. We came very close to winning. Chris, Brian and I coached the team on how to fish the canal and the others listened well and practised. Unfortunately one of our best anglers was forced to drop out of the team on the evening before the match. The only available reserve had never, ever, fished the canal, but now he had no choice. He came last in his section, while the angler next to him won the whole match; we then lost the team event by an odd couple of points. Without the forced substitution we would have won.

We also entered the NFA's knock-out cup. The early rounds were on a regional basis, so that teams did not have to travel far; we managed to draw away to Newton Abbott! They knocked us out on two clay pits, with the unlikely names of 'tip-top' and 'rub-a-dub'.

The following season we progressed further in the same competition, knocking out one of the more powerful Swindon teams in the process, on the Thames at Kelmscott, where Brian and I finished second and first individually. We were eventually knocked out by Bathampton, whom we took to the Gloucester Canal, as we felt that they were far too strong for us on rivers. It almost worked, and I won the match by some distance, but teamwise they beat us by a very narrow margin.

Our big hope for 1982 was the division two national. Our failure to get promoted on the Leeds and Liverpool Canal did have the bonus of leaving us in a division which was competing on the Bristol Avon. If our team was going to do well in any national, this had to be the one.

We finished twenty-ninth. It was a very disappointing result and I took the decision that it was my last national for Isis. I was still a member of a successful six-man team, which made failure at twelve-a-side level more difficult to accept. Fortunately, however, success with a twelve-man team was just around the corner: enter the Stanley Falcons!

## STANLEY FALCONS

The Stanley Falcons team was simply an amalgamation of the Leonard Stanley club side and the Falcons match group. This enabled us to take part in twelve-a-side team events, our main target being the West Wiltshire division of the *Angling Times* winter league. This league was based around venues on the Bristol Avon and we fancied our chances.

During our first attempt to win this league we had a desperate battle with Chippenham, which saw us enter the final round (on the Avon at Bathford) level on points. The tension was unbelievable; but the determination and belief present in the team was phenomenal, and we expected to win.

The river was rain-affected and consequently was not going to be easy, as I soon found out. My peg was full of snags on the inside, so I could only fish a feeder down the middle. For the first one and a half hours I was biteless, then I caught a gudgeon – the blank was

avoided. The next bite came after another hour and resulted in a 5oz dace, which was sure to be worth a few section points, conditions were that bad. After three and a half hours the third and final bite was indicated. This time my heart beat increased as I found myself attached to something more powerful. A 1lb chub resulted and I had done enough to win my section.

The rest of the team had also stood up to the pressure and we won, putting ourselves through to the semi-final, against the other league winners.

Sadly, that was where our challenge faltered. The match was held on the Gloucester Canal, but was preceded by such terribly cold weather that hardly anything would feed. I sat in the middle of a row of nine blanks and despite some good performances from other team members, we missed out on a position in the top four, which was required to go on.

The captaincy of this team was still carried out in the comparatively loose style which had worked so well at six-a-side level. Looking back now, I am surprised that we avoided severe disruption from anglers who were left out of teams, as we had more than twelve members.

At the start of the next season (1983), a very important team event appeared on the match calendar, and was scheduled to take place on the Gloucester Canal: the Clive Smith memorial. Clive had been so popular that the event attracted a huge entry of six-man teams. We fielded two teams, with the 'A' side comprising Brian Pollard, Chris Jurevicius, Andrew Jones, Russ Baker, Brian Wiltshire and me.

Chris and Andrew both caught double-figure weights, to win their sections. I caught double-figures to finish third in mine, and Russ and Brian Pollard both finished very high in theirs. The only comparatively poor result was from the usually very reliable Brian Wiltshire. Our joint performances meant that we finished in second place, beaten only by the England International team, though we managed to beat many other big name teams.

Later that season we had to defend our West Wiltshire winter league title. But this time we started with a disaster on the river Frome, where we finished almost last. We gradually recovered through the rest of the series and ended in second place, but we had given Chippenham too much of a head start at the beginning.

That winter league series was the last time that I fished for Stanley Falcons: I was on the move again, this time to Gloucester United Anglers.

## GLOUCESTER UNITED ANGLERS

There were two reasons for the move. The Gloucester team had been trying to persuade me to join them for some time, but I had not been convinced that it was a move up, rather than sideways. However, they had finished second in the previous season's division one NFA national, and now included both Max Winters and Tony Davis in their line-up, who had both been fishing for other national teams before.

The fact that the team had proved itself to be competitive in nationals was certainly an attraction. I had decided after my national appearances with Swindon Isis that nationals were an expensive waste of time and money unless you were involved with a team capable of winning.

The second reason for moving concerned the area in which Gloucester United usually competed. I had become increasingly frustrated by the lack of press coverage given to matches in my area. The Gloucester Canal was all right, but winning matches on the Bristol Avon or upper Thames was only attracting tiny mentions in the papers: I needed to fish more towards the Midlands in order to attract publicity. Gloucester competed in the West Midlands winter league, so as well as moving to a better side, I would be fishing in a more 'fashionable' area.

The captain at Gloucester United was Terry Gardner, whose leadership qualities were among the best I have ever fished under, and are definitely worth a mention. Terry's job was not an easy one, since the squad included a lot of talented individual anglers, who often had their own strong opinions about what should be happening. They were also drawn from quite a large area. The better a team becomes, the further anglers are willing to travel to become part of it.

Terry had excellent organizational skills, which meant that everyone always knew what was going on, and we were always in the right place at the right time. But more importantly, he was extremely good at handling any moans or disagreements regarding who was in the team, practice sessions, and so on.

Some captains get very annoyed if their decisions are questioned. Many dismiss protests without considering them, which leads to resentment, so is no good. Terry would listen carefully to any questioning or criticism and then give a logical reply. If he disagreed, he would say so and give his reasons. But he was big enough to change his mind if the point put to him was valid. This made Terry a very fair captain, but at the same time he was very firm – he knew how to jump on anyone who was disrupting the team effort. This rare combination of leadership qualities earned him the respect of the team.

### My First Division One National

Our first major challenge of the 1984 season was the NFA south-west regional championship on the Bristol Avon above Bath (I wanted to get away from the Bristol Avon, but this was an exception). We won easily, which set us up nicely for the division one national which was coming up a couple of weeks later, on the River Nene.

I had never even seen the Nene before, but with so many experienced anglers in the side, that was not going to be a problem. The presence of top-quality, highly experienced anglers (Tony Davis and Max Winters in particular), meant that information was no longer the problem which it had been in some of my earlier teams.

It is also worth mentioning the other beneficial effect which the presence of top anglers can have on a team. They can be the source of great inspiration, which can motivate other team members, and consequently influence the whole team's performance in a positive way. On the other hand, top anglers who lack commitment to their team and start to let the side down, will have a very damaging, negative effect on the squad.

Our first visit to the Nene was on the 'north bank' stretch. My draw was greeted by laughs from locals, though they would not tell me why. I soon found out. The first hour was fine and I caught a few fish on a waggler, then along came a boat with a water-skier on tow. As he reached me, the skier let go of the rope and started treading water; the boat then turned around and collected him on the way back. This went on all day; no wonder the locals had laughed – it is not easy to catch with a water-skier splashing around your float.

Subsequent visits to the 'natural' stretches of the river were more successful. The highlight for me was being placed second in one of the giant open matches, with 12lb 1oz of roach and chub. I was happy with the venue and looking forward keenly to my first ever division one national.

On the day of the big match I drew a section on the 'natural' river. I was happy with that, and decided to base my attack on a big stick-float, fished down the middle of the river.

This choice of tactics resulted in a small roach on my first ever cast in division one. By the end of the first hour I had twenty-eight in the net, but the swim then died dramatically, and I struggled for the rest of the event. I suspect that pike or zander may have been responsible for the sudden disappearance of my quarry. By the end of the match I had managed to accumulate around seventy small fish, which weighed 3lb 7oz, scoring fifty-seven points. Most of the other team members had also scored well, so we were going to finish well up.

The results were agonizing. The top ten were read out in reverse order. Tenth, ninth and eighth were read out, and we were not amongst them. Neither were we seventh, sixth or fifth; if we avoided fourth, we would at least get a medal. Then it was announced that there was a tie on points for third place and that it had to be decided on weight. The tie involved us, and we lost out on the total weight: it was a huge disappointment.

Later in the season we took on Shakespeare in the West Midlands winter league and led them for the first three rounds, before eventually finishing second.

At the end of the season our results had been short of spectacular, but were promising enough for us to be optimistic about our chances in the future.

During the close season we carried off the six-a-side Exeter Canal team championships, with a side comprising Brian, Chris, Andrew, Adrian Davies, Max Winters and myself. It was nice to be fishing alongside such a big name as Max: I could remember a time, some years earlier, when it was difficult to pluck up the courage to even go to talk to him.

## My Second Division One National

Our first challenge for the following (1985) season was the division one national on the Leeds and Liverpool canal.

Small canals were almost certainly the team's weakest type of venue. Most of the anglers were far stronger on rivers, so practice was very important.

The canal turned out to be less prolific than it had been four years earlier, when I had made my national debut on it. The tench were starting to decline, and could no longer be relied upon to show almost everywhere. However, there did seem to be more skimmers and perch present, and these could be caught on various maggot baits (bloodworms were banned), but not on casters, which were still preferred for tench. It seemed obvious to me that casters were unreliable and sure to lead to some blowouts; my opinion was overruled by the majority of the side, however, who decided that casters were still the best bait.

I fished the match with squatts and gozzers for hookbait, to finish with seventy-four points, for sixth in my section. That was the top score in the team, and I did not have a single tench in my weight. The casters failed to work properly for the others and we slumped to twenty-sixth place. I still think that we would have been very dangerous if the team had employed my tactics.

The next major team event offered us an easy chance to bounce back with a win: the south-west regional championship was being held on the Gloucester Canal. I was one of many section winners in our successful defence of the title, and we won by a wide margin.

### The 1985 NFA Knock-Out

1985 also found me participating, reluctantly, in the NFA knock-out competition. I was reluctant because I have never been impressed with the tiny, weekend matches which the event involved. It was eight-a-side, so plenty of time and effort were required to fish a sixteen-peg match which would often clash with a much larger, more appealing competition.

Anyway, despite my distaste for the format, we won our way through to the semi-finals, held on the Thames at Wallingford. We were just one step from an expenses-paid holiday to fish the final. Our opponents were Isfield.

The river was low and clear, which meant that odd chub, on a feeder fished well over, were the target. It would be important to catch early, as they had always died in the second half of our practices. Half-way through, our position was looking excellent: we had a comfortable lead and everyone had stopped catching, as predicted. What we had not allowed for were the two large barbel which both fell to Isfield anglers late in the match, but the result still looked close.

The weigh-in was nerve-racking. We had some good weights, headed by my second-placed 9lb 4½oz and Terry Gardner's third-placed 8lb 3oz. But we did not have quite enough to compensate for the two barbel: we were out of the cup.

That left the West Midlands winter league as our final target for the season. Our strong challenge to the Shakespeare team was once again unsuccessful, though I had the consolation of framing three times during the series, so I was happy that I had not let the side down.

### The End of Gloucester United

Then the team was hit by a bombshell. Gloucester United Anglers decided to pull out of the NFA, which meant that the team would not be able to enter NFA events – including the national. Most of the team members attended the AGM where the decision was taken, but abstained when the vote was made. If the various non-match fishing club members were so keen to pull out, it would have been pointless to try to stop them: that would only have caused a terrible relationship between the team and the other club members.

However, I still feel that the decision was a bad one. The main reason for withdrawing appeared to be a financial one, with club members pointing out that NFA membership was costing something like £1 per member, per year. Even now I have trouble understanding how anyone can complain about paying such a tiny figure: I am sure that most of the members who turned up to vote must have spent far more than £1 on petrol and drinks that evening. I found the situation a little illogical.

This was also a time when angling was coming under more attack from various anti-angling groups. I felt that it was rather short-sighted to withdraw support from our national body at a time when angling was under threat, and we needed someone to speak up for us.

## GORDON LEAGUE

I was still contemplating the situation when I

had a phone call from Phil Stone. Phil was captain of the Gordon League team, who at that time were very much a second-rate side. They had suffered from the age-old problem that their best anglers were always pinched by the top local team, Gloucester United in this case. Now there was no Gloucester United and Phil was both ambitious enough and sharp enough to try to take advantage of the situation. We arranged to meet to discuss the possibility of me and other members of the now extinct Gloucester team joining Gordon League.

There was a limit to how many new anglers would be able to join. It was going to be a difficult balancing act: too many and the existing Gordon League members would not accept the changes: too few, and the team would still not be strong enough to win.

Eventually we went for the younger element of the Gloucester United team, which meant me, Chris Jurevicius, Brian Polland and Andrew Jones, who were still fishing together after all those changes from one team to another. Tom Price also moved to Gordon League with us; his brother Tony was already in the squad so Tom would fit in easily.

I think it is fair to say that our arrival triggered off huge enthusiasm within the existing squad. Suddenly, after years of struggling, they felt that they could win. There was precious little bad feeling from anglers who must have been concerned at losing their place, and the team gelled together into a strong unit very quickly. What we needed now was an important team match to go after – we had an NFA national.

**The 1986 Division Four National**

Gordon League's consistent failure to make an impression in previous nationals meant that they were firmly embedded in division four. The 1986 division four event was on the River Witham. Most of us had never seen the venue before, but that was only regarded as a minor detail, which we would overcome.

The whole squad travelled to the Witham for several open matches, and we came away from them with some successes. We sorted out how to catch eels on the pole and roach at half-depth, on the waggler. We also discovered that in the early sections bloodworms were a more reliable approach on the pole than the maggots for eels. We broke the methods down to very simple ones; if we had talked about lots of options and complicated the situation, I think that some team members would have struggled.

Owing to Gordon League's lack of success in previous Nationals the bookmakers were offering us quite generous odds. So, by the time I boarded my section coach, I had lent the bookmakers quite a lot of my hard-earned cash. I was very confident that we would do well, and showing the less experienced members of the team that I was happy to risk my money on their ability, hopefully reinforced their self-belief.

I had drawn the end section at Langrick, a stretch which I had not practised on. As we started walking along the bank to our pegs, two things struck me. The water was extremely clear, and the wind had got up and was blowing with considerable force straight down the river.

I was some distance from the bridge in an area with no shelter at all. Then, as I got closer to my peg I noticed something else. The gin-clear water looked strangely dark for some distance out from the bank. As I reached my swim I realized what the dark patch was: a huge weed-bed, stretching a long way from the bank for three pegs, of which mine was the middle one.

I dragged my pole from the holdall and assembled it. I wanted to establish whether I could reach past the weed. The longest length I owned at that time was 11m, and it was a couple of metres short. Swinging the tackle past the pole end was not an option because of the strength of the wind; this was not even possible with a bottom-end-only float, as the weed came right to the surface.

The height of the weed would also prevent me from sinking the line when fishing a waggler further out. I think I can safely say that this was not one of the easiest pegs that I have ever drawn. Yet it was essential that I caught some fish from it.

I started on a waggler, casting downwind so that the float was under control for a short time before the wind pushed the line in front of it. This quickly produced a roach and a dace for a total weight of about 3oz or 4oz. Then the wind became even worse and the waggler was rendered completely useless. I did try sinking the line, but it tied itself to the weed-beds almost instantly. Then, in the ultra-clear shallow water between me and the start of the weed, I spotted a couple of tiny fish.

I had a pack of bloodworms with me, which our captain had insisted that everyone took, just in case of emergencies. I mixed some with a small quantity of groundbait and dropped it in by the edge of the weed, about 3–4ft (90–120cm) from the bank. More tiny fish appeared. By the end of the match I had swung in about sixty such little roach, but was not very happy – I could see no way that I would score decent points. The scalesman announced a weight of 1lb 8oz; I enquired how many had beaten that in the twenty or so pegs he had already weighed in. 'Only two or three', was the reply. Suddenly life was worth living again.

One of the anglers next to me blanked, the other caught one small eel. I scored fifty-six points which, at the time of writing, is still my lowest ever score in a national; but considering the circumstances, I certainly did not regard it as a failure.

On my arrival back at the headquarters the nail-biting started. One by one the others returned: only one man was in the bottom half of his section, the others all reported results ranging from decent to excellent, with the star performances coming from Robbie Payne with seventy-one points, Ken Burdekin with seventy-two and Brian Pollard with seventy-three.

Trev's won, but we finished second and collected silver medals, plus a few pounds from the bookie and a huge boost to the team's already high morale.

## The End of My Time with Gordon League

Our next main challenge was the West Midlands winter league, an event in which Gordon League traditionally finished close to last. 1986 was a bit different.

The first round was on the Warwickshire Avon at Charlton and Cropthorne. Shakespeare's team weight was 35lb; we managed 51lb, to win by a mile, and I experienced a very enjoyable day as I contributed over 27lb of our total. The whole squad was jumping up and down with delight after that one; but, over the series, Shakespeare's consistency proved too much for us and we eventually had to settle for second in the league. Considering some of the teams we beat, that was no disgrace.

The following season we started well again. We fielded the top two teams in both the Exeter Canal team championships and the Turner 400, on the Thames. We also finished as runners-up in the Clive Smith memorial on the Severn, fishing from the next peg to Shakespeare (we enjoyed that).

Our national was also on the Severn and once again we broke our approach down into some very simple but reliable methods. We all but ignored the barbel, which most people were getting excited about, and concentrated on chub, eels and bleak. We finished third and collected medals again.

True team spirit is difficult to obtain, particularly in large squads, but Gordon League had it. Unfortunately, my time with them was to end abruptly. As well as team successes, I had consistently continued to add to my list of individual results and this attracted the attention of the Shakespeare team. In October 1987 I was offered a place in the superteam's line-up: it was the kind of offer which could not really be refused. Once again I was on the move.

The move came as no surprise to my Gordon League team mates. Many of them could not understand why Shakespeare had not approached me several years earlier; they also realized that I could not turn the opportunity down, so we parted on friendly terms.

## SHAKESPEARE SUPERTEAM

So started a four-year stay with the superteam, a side which tended to rely more on individual flair than on practice and carefully thought-out and reliable, team approaches.

When I joined there were some very talented anglers in the team, but I lived in a different area to many of them and they were not particularly familiar with my results. The team members who I had fished against the most were Tony Davis and Maurice Dutfield, and these were the two who pushed hardest for my inclusion, as they were well aware of my track record. I remain indebted to them both.

I think it's fair to say that some of the others who did not know me so well, would have preferred new members from their own areas. This meant that I was not welcomed with quite as much enthusiasm from some quarters as I could have hoped for. However, I am not easily deterred, and set about establishing myself as an important part of the team.

One year later my results had done the talking for me, and I was firmly established as a member of the team on virtually all types of venue. Such was my success that Ken Giles, the captain who had originally been brave enough to go along with Tony and Maurice's recommendation of me, started enquiring if they had any more potential superteam anglers hidden up their sleeves.

There were far too many team events during my time with Shakespeare for me to try and cover every one, so I will settle for a few of the most memorable.

### The 1989/90 Super League

The biggest win during my involvement with Shakespeare has to be the first ever super league event, in the 1989/90 season. Our progress through to the final was hard work. Our

division included Starlets, who used a large squad, including a number of specialists, to increase their chances on the varied programme of venues.

We won the first round, but then fell behind and were still trailing with just one round left. I cannot remember the exact gap, but it was in the region of fifteen points (the league was decided on accumulative section points).

The last round was on the Warwickshire Avon, at Twyford Farm, a venue which suited us: so the scene was set for a nail-biting showdown. We put on a powerful display and managed to overtake our competitors with several points to spare, consequently securing our place in the semi-final. This found us up against Isfield and Daiwa Gordon league, on the Thames at Medley (Oxford) and on the Oxford Canal at Kirtlington.

The river leg was first, and it was on a venue which suited our talented river anglers. We built up a big points lead, with Dave Harrell and I leading the way, to take on to the canal. The second leg was short on fish, but we managed to win again, against opposition who, like us, could not claim many canal experts within their ranks. The semi-final had been somewhat easier than the division.

The other semi-final winners were Daiwa Trent men; so we faced them in the final, which was to be fished in southern Ireland. The finals format of a pole match, a feeder match and a waggler match on three different venues, had to be changed slightly, as two of the three intended venues were all but fishless when we practised. The three different methods were eventually all fished on one reasonably prolific water; we won very easily.

This was the first major national team title that I had ever been involved in winning and consequently is one which I will always remember. Our victory was a result of the impressive individual talent which the team contained. This talent could shine in a situation where extensive practice was out of the question, and the result was largely decided on pure fishing ability (this was the case in Ireland).

However, due to the more 'professional' hard-working approaches which were being developed by some other sides, we were being caught up. This was not helped by our having a comparatively small squad: if several anglers were off-form, or not putting in enough effort or practice, they could not all be dropped.

### The Problem with Canal Events

In the following season's super league, Starlets beat us for the division. Our failure was largely down to our lack of experienced canal anglers: we were often walking on a tightrope when we came up against strong canal teams. Most of the squad members had a strong preference for river matches, which meant that we often fielded canal sides which included one or two men who did not really want to be there. The current Shakespeare team has worked hard to correct this situation.

There were notable exceptions to this attitude towards canals. The 1988 winter league semi-final, held on the Grand Union Canal near Northampton, is an excellent example. On that occasion extensive practice and a lot of determination led to a superb team performance, which saw us safely through to the final.

We also won the following season's semi-final, on another stretch of the Grand Union Canal at West Drayton. But, strangely, far less effort went into that match and we can thank several inspired performances (from individual winner, Maurice Dutfield, in particular) for that triumph.

The finals were another matter. We reached two of them during my four years with the team, but failed to make any real impact. Both were on Mallory Park Lakes, and I think I am right in saying that practice was not allowed, so teams which were used to the type of fishing required (mainly carp) took some beating. At that time few of our squad members, including me, had any extensive knowledge of carp fishing.

### The 1988 John Smith's Event

Another team event in which we did achieve great success, was the annual John Smith's team event on the Warwickshire Avon at Evesham. I was not included in the 1988 team, but appeared on the next three occasions in this six-a-side (and more recently five-a-side) event and was on the winning side each time.

There was very strong competition for places in this line-up, on what was basically a home water. Everyone in the team that was eventually chosen knew what they were doing and, more importantly, were 100 per cent committed to the task of winning. The attitude for this event was always superb and our results, against strong opposition, showed it. I played my part in the victories with two section wins and a second in my three appearances.

### The NFA Nationals

The NFA nationals which I fished with Shakespeare were not quite so successful. When I joined, the team was working its way up through the divisions and was residing at the time in division three.

In 1988, division 3 was held on the Leeds and Liverpool Canal. I cannot get away from the place. Every team I join seems to have a national there. You will remember that when I fished there in 1985 for Gloucester United, the fishing was on the decline: by 1988 it was worse. The marginal weed, which had lined the canal on both banks in the early 1980s, had now all but vanished, and so had the tench. The quality of fishing in many areas could now be politely described as poor.

The main priority for the team was to get to division one as quickly as possible, so we spent a limited amount of practice time on the water. It was enough to accomplish our mission, as we were safely promoted, finishing in fourth place, though that position was a touch disappointing: a medal would have been nice.

The following year we did manage a medal, for third place on the Huntspill and Kings

Sedgemoor Drain. This result also meant that division one had been reached: we were ready to do battle in the top flight, on the Witham, in 1990.

We knew that bloodworms and jokers were likely to play an important part in this Witham national, but out practice with them was handicapped when we were severely short-measured by our supplier. We did spend several days on the water, but no solid team plan emerged, and we went into the match relying largely on individual ability to see us through.

My own match was an interesting one. I fed jokers in leam at about 13m (that range was necessary to get past extensive shallows) and also fed five or six balls of groundbait two-thirds of the way across, in case of bream. I then started with a whip, fishing with blood-worms, not far past the marginal weed. The inside line produced several tiny fish, but then died. A switch to the long pole also produced for a short time but then that, too, dried up. Not quite the start I had hoped for. I continued to switch between the two areas for the first hour, with little success. However, by this time I had seen several bream caught to my left. Not right next to me, but close enough to be of interest.

I analyzed the situation. There were four hours left and bream were obviously feeding in the area: if I went for them could I be almost certain to catch one? The answer was 'yes': it was a calculated gamble, made easier by my lack of action on the pole.

I picked up a leger rod and lobbed an open-end feeder on to my pre-baited area. For the next one and a half hours I caught nothing: but I was getting line bites, so fish were definitely in the peg. Then I caught one, though not a very big one – probably 1½lb – so my tactics were justified. During the next two and a half hours I picked up five more of various sizes, to finish with 14lb 12oz. That was enough for me to finish in the section money, and I was also top scorer for the team.

The rest of the team had not done badly either, considering that we had not really sorted it out, and we finished in fifth place. If our practice had run more smoothly, I suspect that we could have ended with medals.

The 1991 division one event was on a venue which was far less promising from our team's point of view: the Trent and Mersey Canal. The reservations about canal matches resurfaced, and I think few squad members expected us to figure prominently in a match which involved some very good specialist canal teams. Once negative thoughts set in, a team is usually in trouble.

Personal pride meant that I spent enough time on the canal to become happy with it and, on the day of the race, I was pleased to be top points-scorer for the team again. On the team front, however, we had a very mixed set of results, ending in a perfectly respectable position, though we never looked like challenging for a medal. I had no idea at the time that this was destined to be my last national appearance for the Shakespeare superteam.

## VAN DEN EYNDE ESSEX

A few weeks later I received a phone call from one Peter Clapperton, who explained that he wanted to revive Essex County's flagging performances by introducing more top anglers. He had already signed up Peter Vasey and Derek Young from Trevs Browning, and was looking for two more: Wayne Swinscoe and myself, from Shakespeare.

This approach came entirely out of the blue, and caught me by surprise, leaving me with a big decision to make. We spoke for the first time, on a Monday. On the Tuesday I tried, unsuccessfully, to contact Ken Giles, so that I could discuss the situation with him. Imagine my surprise when I picked up the *Angling Times* on the Wednesday morning to find that the story was front page headlines: Peter had told the press before asking me! He certainly knew how to get publicity. I suspect that Ken must have got a surprise as well when he picked up his paper.

The decision was not one to be rushed. Shakespeare were still a very big name, bigger than Essex at the time. I had to decide whether Peter's very ambitious plans for his side would work. During the course of five days I spoke to a number of people about the situation, including Bob Nudd, Wayne Swinscoe, several of my Shakespeare team mates and Peter Clapperton himself (with lots of questions). Eventually I decided it would work, so agreed to join: Wayne came to the same decision.

Peter explained the view that the team would take a couple of years to gel together well enough to win big titles. He was to be proved wrong, for the newly named Van Den Eynde Essex were to hit the headlines very quickly.

There was only one major team competition left in the 1991/92 season after the team was rebuilt: the *Angling Times* winter league. Essex compete in the Cambridgeshire division. We won it, and so found ourselves in the semi-final against all the other divisional champions from the southern half of the country. A strange twist of fate had decreed that this match was on the Gloucester Canal: I was naturally expected to play an influential role in the event.

History shows that we were the victors by a comfortable points margin over second-placed Avon Bait, a result which generated even greater enthusiasm among an already fired-up squad. We were thus through to the final at Roundhay Park in Leeds, where some carefully worked-out approaches, and a great deal of determination, made the title ours.

It was definitely another performance to remember with great pleasure. We had finished fourteen points clear of our nearest challengers, with a score which included section wins from Bob Nudd, Martin Bull, Peter Clapperton and me. Anyone who had doubted the new-look Essex team's ability to win, needed to rethink.

For the 1992/93 season we targeted both the *Angling Times* winter league and the Drennan super league. We also entered the NFA knock-out cup, with a view to taking it one step at a time. This format is very difficult to fit into a hectic season, but we managed to squeeze all

*Another bloodworm-caught fish is eased into the landing net on the Gloucester Canal.*

of the rounds in and made it through to the final: here we were very disappointed to be beaten into second place in a match where our team filled the top three individual places.

To finish as runners-up in a national competition is still a very good performance, but it is the winners who are remembered: so success in the two leagues became important.

We did consider the NFA national championships, but the 1992 event was simply not on a particularly favourable venue for us (the Trent), and we decided to put virtually no effort into it, so that we could concentrate on winning our targeted events. If you try to win too much you can end up failing in everything, because the team's time and effort are split too many ways.

### The 1992/93 Drennan Super League

The super league was to be a very tough

struggle. The south-east division contains some very good teams, including Dorking, and they led us for most of the series. With just two rounds left they were over twenty points clear, but it was not enough: two strong performances by Essex on those vital last two matches (particularly on the Lea at Enfield Lock) swung the league round in our favour. We scraped home to win a place in the semi-finals.

The semi-final became virtually a two-horse race. The reigning champions – team Tubertini from St Helens, and ourselves finished a long way clear of the rest on the two-leg event, which took place on the Cam and Grand Union Canal. We won the first leg, while they won the second: there was not much between the teams, with Tubertini just edging in front over the two days. The Tubertini organization, determination and team spirit was impressive, and we knew that the three-leg final in Ireland would be a very tough challenge.

It was. But we pulled through, with Pete Vasey playing a crucial role. Pete only fished in the pole leg of the final (each of the three days is limited to one method – pole, running-line float and leger), but the tactics which he sorted out gave us a big lead.

The venue, Garadice Lake, was very clear, which meant that the fish were not very enthusiastic about swimming close to the bank, within pole range. Pete solved the problem by fishing a 2 swanshot waggler on a long line, with a 12.5m pole. This set up enabled him to fish well past the range which could be achieved by more conventional tactics.

Tubertini had not worked out that method and consequently we won the first match by twenty-seven points. Barring disasters that was always going to be a winning lead. The men from St Helens, however, did not give up and beat us narrowly in both of the other legs, but we still won by a twenty-point margin. This was our second major national title.

## The 1993 *Angling Times* Winter League

In the same season we also successfully navi-

*Derek Young with his winning catch from the first day of the 1993 Drennan super league final in Ireland.*

gated our way back to the winter league final to defend that title. The 1993 event was to be on the River Trent in Nottingham, on the embankment stretch. This length is pleasure-fished so heavily that we had to meet on the bank at 6 a.m. when practising, in order to be certain of securing pegs!

The squad's three-day practice stint sorted out two main methods which were very productive: the block-end feeder fished with maggots down the middle of the river, and the pole fished in conjunction with bloodworms.

We were amazed at just how many quality roach we could catch on bloodworms and thoroughly expected our approach to have a major impact on the river's matches. But it was not to be. On the day of the match the method caught only small fish from a river which produced less fish than expected all round. We finished a disappointing fourth: close to second, but a long way behind the winners, DELCAC, who attacked the water with open-end feeders and casters, a method which all of the other teams had ruled out as a non-starter.

We lost on that occasion, but the fact remains that I now fish for a team which is winning national titles, a big change from the early days, when local team matches were the target. But the correct attitudes and approaches to succeed at team fishing are very similar at all levels.

## ESSENTIALS FOR SUCCESSFUL TEAM FISHING

To start with, a good team spirit is essential. It is vital that the squad works together as a unit: sharing knowledge and helping each other, despite competition for places in the team which is eventually picked. The situation within Van Den Eynde Essex is a strange one, with a few anglers being paid to compete for the team, whilst most are not: this could easily lead to internal tensions, but does not appear to. The team spirit remains intact.

If a team is to win on a regular basis a good deal of determination is also required. Good teams enjoy winning, but also realize just how much effort is necessary, and are prepared to put it in. Practice and preparation are essential.

A large squad can also help the situation: competition for places can be a great motivator, and a large squad also allows for comparatively specialized anglers, who are vital on some venues, but of limited use on others.

High-quality leadership is, of course, also important to a top team. A good leader will ensure that the team is well prepared for each challenge and he will listen to, and deal with, any complaints or problems which develop within the ranks. He also needs to pick teams without favouritism. Selecting friends, or himself, before other anglers who are performing better, is an excellent way to lose the respect of the squad. He also needs to be continually on the look-out for new anglers to strengthen the squad. Within any team there will always be people stepping down for various reasons: financial problems, marital problems, loss of form, loss of enthusiasm, or a host of other reasons. If these can be replaced with better anglers the team should improve.

A word of warning: some very good individual anglers are not good team men! If drawn on lots of fish they do well, but they are not prepared to 'scratch' on difficult days, or on bad pegs, and consequently let the team down far too often. An angler of slightly less ability, who tries as hard as possible no matter how tough the situation, may be of more use to a team – successful team fishing has got a lot to do with working together.

# 13 SUMMARY

You have now read my methods and ideas on how to be successful at match angling (or angling in general). Hopefully you have now got lots of new ideas buzzing about inside your head; it is up to you to make use of them.

You are obviously interested in improving your own angling – otherwise you would not be reading this to start with – so try out whatever ideas are applicable to the venues that you fish. But try not to expect instant miracles: angling is a sport with so much to learn that nobody ever knows it all. I still pick up new information and ideas every week of each season: if I stop learning my days as a successful match angler will soon be over.

## TRYING OUT NEW IDEAS

I have mentioned earlier in the book, that it is wise to ask other people for advice, and also to share ideas with friends in order to learn faster. It is also a good idea to try out new ideas of your own, or from books, whenever you go pleasure fishing. If you often go pleasure fishing to the same places and always fish in the same manner, because you know that you will catch some fish, you are learning little or nothing. It is far more constructive to try out different ideas, whether it concerns different hooks, different feeding patterns, baits, floats, using poles instead of rods, or anything else. Some ideas will fail, others will be very successful, and once you start to find these successful methods your match results, confidence and enjoyment should all increase.

My own pleasure fishing would be far more accurately called practice fishing. I rarely go fishing just to catch a few fish, I am always looking to learn. The mental challenge of angling is one of the main attractions for me. I always think carefully about what I am doing and try to understand why a method works, until eventually it becomes possible to have a better understanding about what is happening beneath the surface of the water you are fishing.

From a very young age my practice always had some purpose to it. When I was at school my choice of venues was very limited, to say the least, and largely revolved around the local lake. I would deliberately fish as many areas as possible – rather than stick to the hot spots – and would try out quivertipping and swingtipping despite the fact that they were not good methods for the venue. At least when I was taken to club events on waters where legering was important, I had some basic knowledge of what to do. Various combinations of groundbaiting and loosefeeding were also tried out, while maggots, bread and worms were all experimented with as baits.

My enthusiasm in those days was so great that I would sometimes get up at 4 a.m., walk to the lake, fish for several hours and then come home and go to school! In the evening I would often go fishing again: I have no idea where I used to get the energy from to do that.

Another of my early venues was a very small concrete reservoir, which contained masses of tiny, stunted carp. These fish were usually caught on little pieces of breadpunch, and were so shy that ultra-delicate floats had to be developed in order to catch heavily – something which had never been vital when fishing for the much larger fish in my local lake.

I also used these tiny carp to start experi-

*Dexterity is required when manoeuvring long poles.*

menting with bloodworms. In winter they became virtually uncatchable on bread so hardly anyone fished for them. However, I had read about bloodworms and had managed to find some in a local pond, so I started to try them under winter conditions. The difference was incredible. Instead of struggling for a bite I would catch around fifty fish in a session – I was benefiting from my willingness to experiment.

Whatever stage your fishing is at, never lose sight of the fact that you go fishing to enjoy yourself. I enjoy fishing at a very high level against the anglers at the very top end of the sport, but I am well aware that most anglers are more than happy to compete at club or open-match level. However, for those of you who are particularly ambitious and want to go as far as possible in the sport, I would strongly suggest that you become very confident on your local waters before you start to spread your wings and move further afield. There are few short cuts to the top and progress takes time; so if you find yourself competing at a level which you find too demanding, or too competi-

tive to be fun, or you are always being beaten, drop back down to a slightly lower standard. You can always try moving up again in the future when your own ability has improved, and practising the methods which you are struggling with will help to speed up your improvement.

The difference between winning and losing is very narrow in most sports and angling is no exception. As I mentioned at the start of the book, if you can come up with one extra little idea (whether it involves your tackle or your actual fishing method) that catches one more fish, you will have improved your performance. If you can come up with ten small improvements on what you are doing then you might be able to catch ten more fish, probably a lot more. And ten more fish could certainly be the difference between winning and losing! Virtually everyone who reads it should have picked up a lot more than ten new ideas from this book, so I hope that in future I draw next to plenty of anglers who will not have bothered to read it.

## THE RIGHT TACKLE

As well as understanding what methods need to be employed on a particular day, it is also very important that your tackle is finely tuned for the job. Hooks and lines are the most vital links between you and the fish, so take great care in ensuring that they are not going to let you down.

I always test lines with both a spring balance and a micrometer, to ensure that I know exactly what I am fishing with – some of the labelling on spools is inaccurate, and different batches can vary quite dramatically. I first discovered this problem a long time ago when I suddenly started getting broken by fish, when applying only very modest pressure to them. The hooklengths which I was using were of line which should have been breaking at just over 1lb; tests with a spring balance revealed that the offending spool was breaking at 12oz, while other spools of the same line were breaking at close to 1½lb. So my hooklengths were breaking at around half the strain which I was used to – little wonder that I was being broken.

Hooks are also prone to variation and need to be inspected carefully, though I must say that the general quality of hooks is now very high. Problems which can arise include points which are too fine and consequently bend over, or too soft, allowing them to open out when playing large fish, spades which are too large, which encourages the hook to spin as you wind in or spades which are too small, which can allow the whipping to slide off under pressure. Most of these problems can be picked up by close inspection or tweaking hooks with your fingers to establish whether they are too soft. Close scrutiny takes time, but it is certainly worth it, and will prevent you from losing a number of fish over the course of a season.

Floats do not need to be immaculate to do an efficient job, but they do need to be exactly the right size and shape to perform the function you want them for. Also remember to carry spares; everyone occasionally loses or breaks one during a match, and it is essential that you can quickly retackle with an identical rig.

What I look for in rods and reels I covered in earlier chapters. Your preferences may be different, but looking at which rods and reels anglers like me use, will give you a sound starting point when choosing for yourself. I only use tackle which performs satisfactorily.

## MENTAL ATTITUDE

Another very important aspect of match angling which you will need to work on if you want to become more successful, is concentration and self-belief.

Five hours is an awfully long time, and it is very easy to let your concentration slip. How many times have you watched the bloke next door net a fish, to see how big it is, only to look back to your float just in time to see it reappear, as the fish which has been chewing the bait for several seconds lets go? That fish might have been a match winner, so might the one which you missed while you were pouring a cup of coffee!

Concentration and thought is particularly difficult to maintain when things start to go wrong, and you begin to fall behind the anglers around you. But to become successful it is essential that you hold yourself together and do not give up or panic. Very few matches run totally smoothly, so if you can keep on fishing to the best of your ability, you will still be able to overtake the other anglers on many occasions – they might start well, but if they do slow up, you must be fishing well enough to take advantage and overhaul them.

When the Welsh angler, Clive Branson, won the world championships several years ago, he explained that reading up on how to develop PMA (Positive Mental Attitude) had been a key factor in his success. Some people laughed at this and regarded it as a silly idea: I did not. I have never read up on the subject but I am well aware of just how important it is. The correct mental attitude enables an angler (or any other sportsman) to carry on giving 100 per cent, no matter what goes wrong. For example, losing a large fish at the net can leave some anglers in a terrible frame of mind so they are all but useless for the rest of the event. That is no good; the angler must force himself to keep going and believe that he can still succeed.

The toughest situation, for many, is when they have drawn next to a top angler, whose reputation is such that they decide they have no chance whatsoever of beating him, and give up before the start. I have seen this happen to anglers who have drawn next to me, on many occasions. From my younger days I can remember drawing next to big name anglers myself, and I can still recall the feeling of resignation to being beaten. But I managed to overcome that and learnt how to blinker myself to get on with the job in hand rather than spending all the match worrying about the opposition. Any aspiring match angler needs to develop the same mental concrete barrier.

Remember that even if the star angler next to you fishes brilliantly and wins the match, you can still finish in the prizes by keeping close to him. You do not have to beat him to get a result! That philosophy may help you to cross the barrier. And, if he does beat you, do not forget to go to talk to him straight after the match and learn as much as possible.

## UNDERSTANDING FISH

On the subject of learning as much as possible, I would advise you not to pass up any opportunity to watch fish in the wild, particularly if it is possible to feed them and watch their reactions. This can be a real eye-opener. I also use an aquarium at home to improve my knowledge of how fish behave. Many people keep tropicals, goldfish or exotic salt-water species; I, however, keep roach, gudgeon and ruffe, which is far more interesting! By watching their behaviour, particularly at feeding time, I become more in tune with what is happening beneath the surface when I am trying to catch

their cousins. I am sure that this helps my fishing – it may well help yours!

Another system which I use to some effect involves making notes about successful tactics which have worked particularly well on venues which I do not visit very frequently. Feeding, hooks, floats, shotting, ranges, most successful baits and anything else of use, will all be jotted down on a card for reference, if I return to the venue a year or two later. I tend to remember most details, particularly on venues which I am fishing on a regular basis, but key points of a successful set of tactics can easily fade from the memory after a couple of years. So I use notes as an insurance policy; once again, it may pay you to do the same.

Having the right information and knowing what to do is, of course, a key part of match angling success, and the main reason why very few young superstars appear. If a young angler does make a big name for himself it will nearly always be on a limited number of methods, or venues. Bear this in mind and do not allow yourself to become too disheartened if your progress up the ladder of success seems to be slow.

## LEARNING FROM SUCCESSFUL ANGLERS

Watching top anglers is another way to speed up your progress. The best places to do this are on the big invitation matches, which take place on a number of venues during the summer months. The John Smith's championship, on the Warwickshire Avon at Evesham, is probably the longest running of these. Others include the Van Den Eynde classic at Holme Pierrepont, Nottingham, the Kamasan British Open, which is usually held on the River Trent, and the UK championship, which takes place in four variable venues, usually well spread around the country.

If you go to one of these events to learn, rather than just to have an enjoyable day out, get there before the start and get in position behind one angler who you think that you can learn from. Then stay with that angler for several hours. By doing that, and watching very carefully, you will see how he goes about getting the fish to feed, and what variations in feeding or tactics he employs. If you just wander up and down the bank for the whole match, stopping to watch anyone who happens to be catching, you will learn far less because you will have missed out on the crucial work which will have gone on at the start of the match.

## HANDLING YOUR CATCH

Finally, always remember that fish are living creatures and treat them with the respect they deserve. Unhook them swiftly but carefully, and handle them with due consideration. Make sure that your keepnet is adequately submerged in the water and that it is large enough if you fish venues which throw up huge weights. Then, when the event has finished, and you are going to weigh in, make every effort to avoid rolling the fish down the net. Whenever possible you should grab hold of the bottom of the net and allow the catch to swim towards the top, before lifting them from the water. Damaged fish do not help the image of the sport, so always take great care and set an example to others.

The same applies if you, or anyone else, want to take photographs of the catch. Keep the fish out of the water for as short a time as possible and plan what photos you wish to take in advance, in order to keep the time involved as short as possible.

Match angling is a great sport and has provided me with countless friends and happy memories. But do not forget the importance of looking after the fish, so that we can all look foward to many great days in the future.

*A small fish, but it counts!*

## A FINAL WORD

Here is one final thought on match angling to leave you with: all that matters is what weight of fish you have got in the keepnet at the end of the competition. It does not matter how you caught them. Many anglers forget what they are trying to achieve and spend a lot of time trying to look good rather than putting a weight in the net. For example, it is pointless running a stickfloat perfectly down the inside of a peg all day for 5lb of roach, when the man in the next peg has caught 15lb of chub on a feeder! Never lose sight of what you are trying to achieve, then you will find match angling far easier to master.

# INDEX